Thailand Travel Guide:

Delve into Secret Havens, Savor the Vibrant Street Food, and Experience Local Traditions Just Like a True Thai Local

By
Marlena Brightview

© **Copyright 2024 - All rights reserved.**

The contents of this book may not be reproduced, duplicated, or transmitted without the direct written permission of the author or publisher.

Under no circumstances will the publisher or author be held liable for any damages, recovery, or financial loss due to the information contained in this book. Neither directly nor indirectly.

Legal Notice:

This book is protected by copyright. This book is for personal use only. You may not modify, distribute, sell, use, quote, or paraphrase any part or content of this book without the permission of the author or publisher.

Disclaimer Notice:

Please note that the information contained in this document is for educational and entertainment purposes only. Every effort has been made to present accurate, current, reliable, and complete information. No warranties of any kind are stated or implied. The reader acknowledges that the author is not offering legal, financial, medical, or professional advice. The contents of this book have been taken from various sources. Please consult a licensed professional before attempting any of the techniques described in this book.

By reading this document, the reader agrees that under no circumstances will the author be liable for any direct or indirect loss arising from the use of the information contained in this document, including but not limited to - errors, omissions, or inaccuracies.

Table of Contents

Introduction 5

Chapter 1: Travel Essentials 8

    What to pack. 10
    Practical Information 16

Chapter 2: Must Visit Places in Thailand 24

    Bangkok 24
    Chiang Mai 28
    Phuket 31
    Ayutthaya 34
    Chiang Rai 36
    Krabi: 38
    Sukhothai 41
    Koh Samui: 44
    Koh Tao: 46
    Kanchanaburi 48
    Koh Phi Phi 51
    Koh Tao: 54
    Pai 60

Chapter 3: Itineraries 64

    One week Itinerary 66
    Two weeks Itinerary 68

Chapter 4: Best Restaurants and Cuisine 71

    Key Features of Thai Cuisine: 71
    Popular Thai Dishes: 72

Regional Variations: 74
Restaurants.. 75

Chapter 5: Accommodations in Thailand............................ 78

Chapter 6: Cultural Activities in Thailand........................... 84

Chapter 7: Nightlife And Festivals In Thailand 88

Festivals 91

Chapter 8: Souvenirs And Shopping in Thailand 97

Souvenirs 101

Chapter 9: Tips For Traveling in Thailand 105

Conclusion.. 109

Introduction

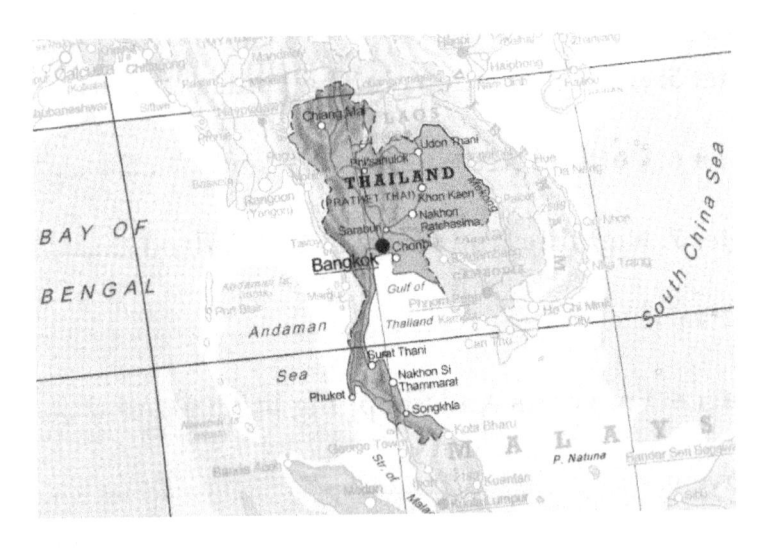

In the heart of Southeast Asia, where vibrant street markets bustle with an intoxicating blend of aromas, and ancient temples whisper tales of empires long gone, lies a land of unparalleled allure. Welcome to the enchanting kingdom of Thailand, a realm where tradition dances gracefully with modernity, and paradise is just a tuk-tuk ride away.

As you step foot on the soil of Thailand, you're entering a world of contrasts and contradictions, where the old and new coexist harmoniously. The hustle and bustle of Bangkok, the capital city, is a perfect reflection of this duality. Skyscrapers punctuate the skyline, casting their long shadows over serene temples adorned with intricate gold leaf designs. Monks clad in saffron robes offer blessings to the devout, while just around the corner, street vendors whip up tantalizing Thai dishes with an aromatic symphony of spices. The city's rhythm is fast, yet there's always time for a traditional Thai smile—a gesture that speaks volumes about the warmth and friendliness of the people.

Venture beyond the urban sprawl, and you'll find that Thailand's beauty knows no bounds. From the tranquil shores of Phuket, where turquoise waters gently lap against pristine beaches, to the verdant northern regions, where rolling hills and lush valleys invite hikers and nature enthusiasts, this country beckons with its unique charm. It's a land where golden palaces, such as the revered Grand Palace in Bangkok, share the spotlight with the simple yet delicious offerings at street food stalls. Every meal is an adventure for the taste buds, a culinary journey that brings you closer to the heart of Thai culture.

Prepare to discover the diverse landscapes, rich history, and warm hospitality of Thailand. Allow this guide to be your passport to a world of towering mountains, mystical islands, and the gracious smiles of its people. Whether you're traversing the bustling streets of Chinatown in Bangkok, exploring the ancient ruins of Ayutthaya, or embarking on a trek through the verdant forests of Chiang Mai, every moment in Thailand promises a new adventure.

With each page, you'll step closer to a realm of beauty, adventure, and culture like no other. Dive into the history of the Thai monarchy, explore the intricate art of traditional Thai dance, and learn about the customs and beliefs that have shaped this nation's character. Discover the intricate practices of Buddhism that have sculpted the country's temples and rituals.

So, dear traveler, fasten your seatbelts, because the journey begins now. Thailand awaits, and your adventure starts here. Whether you're an intrepid explorer seeking off-the-beaten-path experiences or a soul in search of tranquility on pristine beaches, Thailand has a treasure trove of experiences waiting to be unlocked. So, let's embark on this voyage together and let the captivating kingdom of Thailand unfold its wonders before you.

Chapter 1:
Travel Essentials

The best times to visit Thailand considering various factors:

1. **Weather:**
   - **November to February:** This period is the most popular time to visit Thailand because the weather is pleasant. Thailand experiences its cool and dry season during these months. This is perfect for outdoor activities, beach vacations, and exploring cities without dealing with oppressive heat or excessive rainfall.
   - **March to May:** In most of Thailand, these months are considered the hot and dry season. Despite the heat, particularly in the northern and central parts, it's still a popular season to go. The mercury can rise as high as 35°C (95°F). If you can handle the heat and wish to escape the busiest tourist seasons, now is the time to go.
   - **June to October:** This is the rainy season. The heaviest rainfall typically occurs in August and September. While it's not the most popular time to visit, it's an excellent choice for budget travelers. Prices are lower, and you can enjoy fewer crowds, but it's essential to be prepared for occasional heavy downpours and possible disruptions in outdoor plans.
2. **Crowds:**
   - **Shoulder Seasons (October, early November, late February, and March):** These months can be a sweet spot for avoiding the largest crowds. You'll

experience fewer tourists compared to the high season while still enjoying decent weather.
- **High Season (November to February):** Expect larger crowds during this period, especially at major tourist destinations. Accommodation and activity prices are higher, but you're likely to have excellent weather.
- **Rainy Season (June to October):** Crowds are much smaller during the rainy season, making it an excellent choice for those who prefer a quieter experience. However, be aware that some tourist spots and activities may be limited due to weather.

3. **Cost:**
   - **High Season (November to February):** Prices for accommodation, flights, and activities are generally higher during the high season. If you're willing to pay more for better weather and fewer inconveniences, this might be the best time for you.
   - **Shoulder Seasons (October, early November, late February, and March):** These months offer a good balance between reasonable prices and decent weather.
   - **Rainy Season (June to October):** The rainy season often features the lowest prices, making it an attractive option for budget-conscious travelers. You can save on accommodation and take advantage of discounts.

4. **Specific Regions:**
   - **Southern Thailand (e.g., Phuket, Krabi, Koh Samui):** Visit during the dry season (November to April) to enjoy clear skies, sunny days, and calm seas, perfect for beach activities and water sports.

- **Northern Thailand (e.g., Chiang Mai, Chiang Rai):** November to February is a great time to explore the cultural and natural beauty of the region without sweltering heat. December can be especially festive due to holiday celebrations.
- **Bangkok and Central Thailand:** November to February is also ideal for these areas to avoid extreme heat and enjoy comfortable temperatures for sightseeing.

What to pack.

Here's a comprehensive packing list to ensure you have everything you need for a comfortable and enjoyable trip to Thailand:

Clothing:

1. **Lightweight, breathable clothing:** Thailand is hot and humid, so pack lightweight, moisture-wicking clothing such as shorts, t-shirts, and dresses. Opt for loose-fitting, natural fabrics like cotton and linen.
2. **Swimwear:** If you plan to visit the beautiful beaches and islands, swimwear is a must.
3. **Comfortable walking shoes:** Bring comfortable and breathable shoes for exploring cities, temples, and markets. Sneakers, sandals, and walking shoes are good choices.
4. **Sandals or flip-flops:** These are essential for the beach and for keeping your feet cool in the hot weather.
5. **Lightweight long-sleeve shirts and pants:** These can provide sun protection and are useful in areas with mosquitoes or during cooler evenings.

6. **Rain gear:** If you visit during the rainy season, a lightweight rain jacket or poncho can be handy.
7. Dress modestly when entering temples and other sacred buildings. Your shoulders and knees should be covered. Always have a scarf or sarong on hand to use as coverup.
8. sunglasses with a hat Take precautions against the sun's powerful beams.

Accessories:

9. **Backpack or daypack:** Ideal for carrying your essentials during daily excursions.
10. **Money belt or concealed pouch:** These are useful for keeping your valuables safe.

Toiletries and Health:

11. **Sunscreen:** Make sure to bring a high SPF sunscreen to protect your skin from the intense sun.
12. **Insect repellent:** Essential for areas with mosquitoes and other bugs.
13. **Travel-sized toiletries:** Shampoo, conditioner, soap, and other personal hygiene items can be purchased locally, but you may prefer your preferred brands.
14. **Basic first-aid kit:** Band-aids, pain relievers, and any specific medicines you might need.
15. **Hand sanitizer:** Useful for maintaining hygiene while on the go.

Electronics:

17. **Travel adapter:** Thailand uses Type A, B, C, and O electrical outlets, so make sure you have the appropriate adapter for your devices.
18. **Camera and accessories:** Capture your memorable moments, and don't forget spare memory cards and charging equipment.
19. **Smartphone:** Useful for navigation, communication, and currency conversion apps.

Documents and Money:

20. **Passport and copies:** Carry your passport and a few photocopies. Keep one copy separately from the original.
21. **Visa:** Check the visa requirements for your nationality and ensure you have the necessary visa or travel documents.
22. **Travel insurance:** It's wise to have travel insurance that covers medical emergencies, trip cancellations, and lost or stolen items.
23. **Cash and credit/debit cards:** ATMs are widely available, but it's good to have some cash on hand.

Miscellaneous:

24. **Travel guidebook:** A guidebook can be helpful for planning and navigating your trip.
25. **Ziplock bags:** Useful for storing snacks, protecting electronics, and keeping your belongings organized.
26. **Reusable water bottle:** Reduce plastic waste by carrying a reusable bottle.

27. **Travel lock:** Use locks to secure your luggage and lockers in hostels.
28. **Travel pillow and eye mask:** Useful for getting some rest during long journeys.

Remember that packing light is often a good idea, as you can always buy clothing and items in Thailand if needed. Tailoring your packing list to your specific itinerary and activities will help you have a more enjoyable and stress-free trip to Thailand.

Getting there and moving around

Getting to Thailand and moving around within the country is relatively straightforward, with numerous transportation options available. Here's a guide on how to get to Thailand and navigate your way around:

Getting to Thailand:

1. **By Air:** The most common way to reach Thailand is by air, with several major international airports across the country. Suvarnabhumi Airport in Bangkok (BKK) and Don Mueang Airport (DMK) are the primary gateways. Other international airports include Phuket International Airport (HKT), Chiang Mai International Airport (CNX), and Krabi International Airport (KBV). Major airlines from around the world operate flights to Thailand.
2. **Visa Requirements:** To enter Thailand, you could need a visa, depending on your nationality. If a visa is required, check the website of the Thai embassy or consulate in your own country and apply beforehand.

Moving Around Within Thailand:

1. **Domestic Flights:** Domestic flights inside Thailand are practical for long-distance travel. Many airlines fly internal routes linking important cities and tourist hotspots, including Thai Airways, Bangkok Airways, and low-cost airlines like AirAsia and Nok Air.
2. **Trains:** Thailand has a vast rail system that connects the country's numerous areas. Trains are a relaxing and beautiful kind of transportation, especially over long distances. Train operations are overseen by the State Railway of Thailand (SRT). Tickets can be purchased online or at train stops.
3. **Buses:** In Thailand, buses are a popular and affordable mode of transportation. Local buses and air-conditioned luxury VIP buses are both options. Bus tickets can be purchased from travel companies or at bus terminals.
4. **Tuk-tuks and Taxis:** They are readily available in most cities and tourist areas. Always negotiate the fare with the driver before the ride, especially with tuk-tuks.
5. **Songthaews:** These shared pick-up trucks with bench seats are a common mode of transport in many Thai towns and cities. They follow set routes and are an affordable option.
6. **Motorcycles and Scooters:** Renting a scooter or motorbike is popular for exploring islands and less crowded areas. Be sure to wear a helmet and have the proper license.
7. **Boats and Ferries:** In coastal and island regions, boats and ferries are crucial for transportation. They connect mainland Thailand to popular islands like Phuket, Koh Samui, and Phi Phi Islands.

8. **Subway and Skytrain:** Bangkok has a well-developed public transportation system, including the BTS Skytrain and the MRT subway. These are efficient for getting around the city and avoiding traffic.
9. **Motorcycle Taxis:** In many cities, motorcycle taxi drivers offer a quick way to navigate through traffic. Negotiate the fare beforehand.

Tips for Getting Around:

- Learn some basic Thai phrases or have them written down to help with communication, especially in rural areas where English may not be widely spoken.
- Make use of ride-hailing apps like Grab in major cities, which can provide more transparent pricing and convenience.
- Be cautious of scams and overcharging, especially at tourist destinations. Always agree on fares or use a meter in taxis.
- When renting vehicles, ensure you have the appropriate license and that the rental agency provides insurance coverage.

Thailand offers a variety of transportation options to suit different preferences and budgets, making it relatively easy to explore the country. Whether you're traveling within cities, to remote islands, or to neighboring countries, there are practical means to reach your desired destinations.

Practical Information

Language and Communication

In Thailand, the official language is Thai (Siamese), and the majority of the population speaks it as their first language. While visiting Thailand, you'll find that English is widely spoken and understood in tourist areas, major cities, and at many tourist establishments. However, it's essential to understand that the level of English proficiency can vary widely among the local population. Here are some tips for language and communication in Thailand:

1. **Learn Some Basic Thai Phrases:** To communicate more easily and to demonstrate respect for the local culture, it's always a good idea to learn a few fundamental Thai phrases. Salutations, the use of the words "please" and "thank you," and requests for directions are all common expressions.
2. **Use English in Tourist Areas:** Many persons employed in the tourism sector, including hotel workers, restaurant staff, and tour guides, speak English in well-known tourist destinations like Bangkok, Phuket, Chiang Mai, and the major resort districts.
3. **Point and Use Visual Aids:** When all else fails, you can use gestures, pointing, and visual aids like maps or photos on your phone to communicate your needs and questions.
4. **Translation Apps:** Utilize translation apps or language apps on your smartphone to bridge the language gap. These can be particularly helpful in situations where English may not be readily available.

5. **Thai Alphabet:** While it's not necessary to learn the entire Thai alphabet, recognizing some letters can be helpful, especially for reading signs and menus in non-touristy areas.
6. **Respect Local Customs:** Thai culture places a high value on respect and politeness. Always be courteous and considerate when communicating with locals. The famous Thai smile goes a long way in fostering positive interactions.
7. **Learn About Wai:** The traditional Thai greeting, the "wai," involves a slight bow with palms pressed together in a prayer-like gesture. While not required for tourists, understanding the wai and how it's used can be a sign of respect.
8. **Be Patient and Understanding:** Not everyone you encounter in Thailand will speak fluent English, so patience and a friendly attitude are key to successful communication.
9. **Use Public Transportation:** When using public transportation, signs and announcements are often in both Thai and English, making it easier for tourists to navigate.
10. **Get a Local SIM Card:** Having a local SIM card with data can be immensely helpful for accessing maps, translation apps, and communication tools while on the go.
11. **Emergency Phrases:** It's a good idea to know emergency phrases or numbers, including how to say "help" or "emergency" in Thai and the local emergency number (191 for police, 1669 for medical emergencies).

Currency and banking

The official currency of Thailand is the Thai Baht (THB), often abbreviated as ฿ or represented by the symbol ฿. The Thai Baht is further subdivided into satang, with 100 satang equaling 1 Baht.

Here are some key points to know about currency and banking in Thailand:

1. Currency Exchange:

- Currency exchange services are widely available in Thailand, and you can exchange major foreign currencies, such as the US Dollar and Euro, at banks, exchange counters, and ATMs.
- It's often recommended to exchange a small amount of currency at the airport or your point of entry for immediate expenses. However, exchange rates at airport counters may not be as favorable as those in town.

2. ATMs:

- ATMs are prevalent in urban areas and tourist destinations. They typically accept major international credit and debit cards.
- ATMs dispense Thai Baht, and many will give you the option to complete the transaction in your home currency. However, it's usually more cost-effective to select the local currency (Baht) and allow your bank to handle the conversion.
- Be aware that some ATMs may charge additional fees for foreign cardholders. Your home bank may also

charge international withdrawal fees, so check with your bank before traveling.

3. Credit Cards:

- Credit cards are widely accepted in upscale hotels, restaurants, and retail outlets, especially in major cities and tourist areas. Visa and MasterCard are the most commonly accepted cards, while American Express and other cards are less so.
- It's advisable to carry some cash for smaller purchases, local markets, and establishments that don't accept cards.

4. Traveler's Checks:

- Traveler's checks are not as commonly used as they once were, and you may find it challenging to exchange them. It's generally more convenient to use ATMs or credit cards.

5. Banking Hours:

- Banks in Thailand are typically open from Monday to Friday, between 8:30 AM and 3:30 PM. Some branches may close for an hour during lunch.
- Currency exchange counters at major airports and some shopping centers have extended hours, including weekends.

6. Safety and Security:

- Exercise caution when withdrawing cash from ATMs, especially in less crowded or poorly lit areas, to reduce the risk of card skimming or theft.
- It's a good practice to inform your bank of your travel plans to prevent your card from being blocked due to suspicious international transactions.

7. Tipping:

- Tipping is not traditionally a part of Thai culture, but it has become more common in the tourism industry. In restaurants, it's customary to leave a small tip (5-10%) if a service charge is not included in the bill.

It's essential to be aware of the exchange rates and any fees associated with currency conversion when handling your finances in Thailand. Additionally, always be cautious when dealing with money, especially in crowded places, to avoid potential scams or theft.

Safety

Thailand is generally a safe country for travelers, but like any destination, it's important to be aware of potential risks and take necessary precautions to ensure your safety. Here are some tips for staying safe in Thailand:

1. General Safety:

- **Stay Informed:** Before traveling, research the latest travel advisories and current safety conditions for your

specific destinations in Thailand. The political and social situation in some areas can change.
- **Local Laws and Customs:** Familiarize yourself with the local laws and customs. For instance, it's essential to show respect for the Thai monarchy, as disrespect can result in severe penalties.
- **Avoid Political Protests:** Be aware of any political demonstrations or protests in the area and avoid getting involved in them, as they can become unpredictable and occasionally violent.

2. Health and Hygiene:

- **Vaccinations:** Ensure you are up to date on routine vaccines and consider vaccinations for diseases like hepatitis A and B, typhoid, and tetanus. Check with a healthcare provider or a travel clinic for specific recommendations based on your itinerary.
- **Food and Water Safety:** Be cautious about the food and water you consume. Stick to bottled water and eat at reputable establishments to minimize the risk of foodborne illnesses.
- **Mosquito-Borne Diseases:** Thailand is a region where mosquito-borne diseases like dengue and Zika are a concern. Use insect repellent and take precautions to avoid mosquito bites.

3. Transportation Safety:

- **Road Safety:** If you plan to rent a scooter or motorbike, make sure you have the necessary permits, wear a helmet, and drive cautiously. Thai roads can be chaotic, and traffic accidents are relatively common.

- **Public Transportation:** Taxis, tuk-tuks, and local buses are generally safe for getting around, but it's essential to agree on fares beforehand in un-metered taxis and tuk-tuks.
- **Motorcycle Taxis:** Motorcycle taxis are common in cities and can be convenient but exercise caution when using them. Make sure the driver provides a helmet.

4. Personal Safety:

- **Petty Theft:** Like in many tourist destinations, petty theft can be a concern in crowded areas, so take precautions to safeguard your belongings. Use money belts, secure bags, and avoid displaying valuable items openly.
- **Beach Safety:** When swimming in the sea, be cautious of strong currents, particularly during the monsoon season. Always heed warnings and flags posted at beaches.

5. Scams:

- Be cautious of common tourist scams, such as tuk-tuk drivers taking you to overpriced shops, gem scams, and taxi drivers refusing to use the meter.

6. Natural Disasters:

- Thailand is prone to natural disasters such as earthquakes, floods, and tropical storms. Stay informed about local conditions and follow any instructions from local authorities in the event of natural disasters.

7. Emergency Contacts:

- Know the local emergency numbers: 191 for police, 1669 for medical emergencies, and 199 for fire emergencies.

Chapter 2:
Must Visit Places in Thailand

Thailand has a vast range of tourist destinations and attractions, from dynamic cities to breathtaking natural settings. For a wonderful trip, these Thailand attractions are must-see:

Bangkok

Bangkok, the bustling capital of Thailand, offers a rich tapestry of experiences for tourists. From iconic landmarks to hidden gems, here's a look at some of the tourist highlights in Bangkok:

Tourist Highlights:

1. Grand Palace and Wat Phra Kaew (Temple of the Emerald Buddha):

- The Grand Palace, Thailand's Kings' formal palace, is a historical wonder. Beautifully landscaped courtyards, superb architecture, and detailed detailing are all present. Wat Phra Kaew is located inside the palace complex and is home to the Emerald Buddha, the most revered religious figure in Thailand.

2. Wat Pho (Temple of the Reclining Buddha):

- Wat Pho is not just well-known for its enormous reclining Buddha; it is also one of Bangkok's largest and oldest temple complexes. Explore the ornately painted cloisters, breathtaking architecture, and on-site traditional Thai massage classes.

3. Wat Arun (Temple of Dawn):

- This iconic temple, with its central prang (tower) covered in ceramic mosaic tiles, is one of Bangkok's most recognizable landmarks. Climbing to the top of the prang provides breathtaking views of the Chao Phraya River.

4. Chao Phraya River Cruises:

- Exploring Bangkok by boat along the Chao Phraya River offers a unique perspective of the city's skyline and historical landmarks. You can choose from various boat options, including dinner cruises, traditional commuter boats, or scenic canal tours.

5. Khao San Road:

- Khao San Road is a vibrant, bustling street known for its budget accommodations, street food stalls, shops, and a lively atmosphere, especially in the evening. It's a hub for backpackers and travelers looking for a fun and energetic experience.

6. Chatuchak Weekend Market:

- This enormous market spans over 35 acres and houses thousands of stalls selling everything from clothing and handcrafted items to plants and pets. It's a shopping paradise for visitors looking for unique souvenirs and gifts.

7. Jim Thompson House:

- Jim Thompson was an American who played a significant role in reviving Thailand's silk industry. His former residence, now a museum, is a testament to his appreciation for Thai art and culture. The lush gardens and the collection of artifacts make this a peaceful and educational visit.

8. Erawan Shrine:

- The Erawan Shrine is a Hindu shrine in the heart of the city, revered for its four-faced Brahma statue. It's a place of worship and cultural performances, offering a unique glimpse into the spiritual life of Bangkok.

Hidden Gems:

1. Wat Saket (Golden Mount):

- Wat Saket, also known as the Golden Mount, offers an oasis of tranquility in the heart of Bangkok. The 318 steps to the top lead to a panoramic view of the city and a golden chedi (stupa) at the summit.

2. Loha Prasat (Metal Castle):

- A hidden gem within the Wat Ratchanatdaram complex, the Loha Prasat is a rare structure with a distinctive design featuring 37 spires, symbolizing the 37 virtues towards enlightenment in Buddhism.

3. Artist's House (Baan Silapin):

- Located along the Khlong Bang Luang canals, this traditional wooden house hosts puppet shows and offers a glimpse into Thailand's rich artistic and cultural heritage.

4. Pak Khlong Talat (Flower Market):

- This vibrant 24-hour market near the river showcases an array of colorful and fragrant flowers and offers a unique sensory experience, especially early in the morning when the market is most active.

5. Bangkok Art and Culture Center:

- This contemporary art space in the Siam Square area features a rotating array of exhibitions, galleries, and events, making it a hub for local and international artists.

6. Bang Krachao (The Green Lung):

- This undeveloped region, known as Bangkok's "Green Lung," provides a peaceful haven from the bustle of the city. By boat or bicycle, explore the park's lush, urban jungle.

7. Wat Bang Phra:

- Wat Bang Phra is famous for its magical Sak Yant tattooing ceremonies, where devotees receive protective tattoos believed to provide supernatural powers. It's an opportunity to observe a unique aspect of Thai culture.

8. Sathorn Unique Tower (Ghost Tower):

- While not officially open to the public, the abandoned Sathorn Unique Tower has become an attraction for urban explorers, offering stunning panoramic views of the city skyline and the Chao Phraya River.

Exploring these hidden gems in Bangkok provides a deeper understanding of the city's rich history, vibrant arts scene, and cultural diversity, making your visit to the Thai capital all the more memorable.

Chiang Mai

Chiang Mai, in Northern Thailand, is a city with a rich cultural heritage, stunning natural surroundings, and a variety of activities and hidden gems for tourists to explore. Here are some of the top tourist highlights and hidden gems in Chiang Mai:

Tourist Highlights:

- **Old City:** Chiang Mai's historic Old City is surrounded by ancient walls and a moat. Within its confines, you'll find numerous temples, markets, and cultural attractions, making it a great place to explore on foot or by bicycle.
- **Doi Suthep Temple:** One of Chiang Mai's most recognizable temples is Wat Phra That Doi Suthep, which is perched atop a mountain overlooking the city. The temple is a significant Buddhist pilgrimage place and provides stunning city views.
- **Elephant Sanctuaries:** Chiang Mai is known for its ethical elephant sanctuaries, where you can observe, interact with, and even help care for rescued elephants in a responsible and compassionate way.
- **Night Bazaars:** Chiang Mai's night bazaars are famous for shopping, dining, and experiencing the local culture. The Night Bazaar and the Saturday and Sunday Walking Streets are must-visit attractions for shopping and sampling Thai street food.
- **Hill Tribe Villages:** Take a guided tour to visit the traditional hill tribe villages in the surrounding mountains. You can learn about the unique cultures and lifestyles of tribes like the Karen, Hmong, and Lisu.
- **Art and Craft Centers:** Chiang Mai is known for its artistic and creative community. Explore art galleries,

studios, and markets to discover handcrafted goods, textiles, and intricate traditional crafts.
- **Cooking Classes:** Learn the art of Thai cuisine by taking a cooking class. You'll visit local markets, purchase ingredients, and prepare authentic Thai dishes with expert guidance.
- **Biking and Hiking:** The region around Chiang Mai offers excellent opportunities for biking and hiking. Explore the lush countryside, national parks, and the picturesque Mae Sa Valley.

Hidden Gems:

- **Wat Umong:** This forest temple offers a tranquil and serene atmosphere, with tunnels filled with Buddhist proverbs and peaceful meditation spots. It's a hidden oasis within the city.
- **Mon Cham:** Located in the mountains, Mon Cham offers beautiful panoramic views and is a quieter alternative to the more famous Doi Suthep.
- **Huay Tung Tao Lake:** A scenic lake surrounded by mountains, this hidden gem is a great place for relaxation, picnicking, and enjoying local food in a peaceful setting.
- **Wat Palad Temple (Hidden Temple):** Located along the Doi Suthep trail, this temple is less frequented by tourists and offers a peaceful escape for meditation and reflection.
- **Mae Kampong Village:** A traditional hill tribe village known for its homestay experiences and lush greenery. It's a great place to immerse yourself in the local culture.

- **Sticky Waterfall (Bua Thong Waterfall):** Located about an hour's drive from Chiang Mai, this unique waterfall allows you to climb up the multi-tiered limestone formations due to the waterfall's porous nature.
- **Doi Inthanon National Park:** Explore the highest peak in Thailand, Doi Inthanon, and its stunning surroundings, including waterfalls, nature trails, and hill tribe communities.
- **Wiang Kum Kam:** An ancient city submerged in earth for centuries, this archaeological site is now being excavated, providing a glimpse into the history of the region.

Chiang Mai offers a wonderful mix of well-known tourist attractions and hidden gems, making it an ideal destination for travelers looking to immerse themselves in Thai culture, explore the natural beauty of the region, and discover unique experiences beyond the beaten path.

Phuket

The most populous island in Thailand, Phuket, is well-known for its magnificent beaches, exciting nightlife, and a variety of tourist activities. Here are some of Phuket's tourism attractions and undiscovered gems:

Tourist Highlights:

- **Patong Beach:** Patong is Phuket's most famous and busiest beach. It offers a wide range of water sports, beachfront bars, and a vibrant nightlife scene. You can also visit the bustling Patong Night Market.

- **Old Phuket Town:** Explore the historic district of Phuket Town, known for its colorful Sino-Portuguese architecture, vibrant street art, and quaint cafes. Don't miss the Sunday Walking Street Market.
- **Big Buddha:** Visit the 45-meter-tall Big Buddha statue on Nakkerd Hill. It offers panoramic views of Phuket and is a place for reflection and beautiful photos.
- **Wat Chalong:** This is Phuket's largest and most important Buddhist temple. It's a serene and culturally significant place to explore.
- **Phang Nga Bay:** Take a boat tour to James Bond Island (Koh Tapu) in Phang Nga Bay, famous for its unique limestone karst formations rising from the sea.
- **Similan Islands:** A haven for divers and snorkelers, the Similan Islands are a group of islands known for their crystal-clear waters and vibrant marine life. Liveaboard diving trips are popular for exploring this underwater paradise.
- **Phuket FantaSea:** Enjoy a cultural theme park with a buffet dinner, live performances, and a blend of Thai culture and mythology.
- **Phi Phi Islands:** Go on a day trip or an overnight stay to the Phi Phi Islands, known for their breathtaking beaches, crystal-clear waters, and vibrant nightlife.

Hidden Gems:

- **Freedom Beach:** This secluded beach is tucked away from the crowds, accessible by a short jungle hike. It's a tranquil place to relax and enjoy the natural beauty.
- **Promthep Cape:** While it's not exactly hidden, Promthep Cape offers stunning sunset views, and the

nearby Windmill Viewpoint is a quieter spot to enjoy the scenery.
- **Laem Singh Viewpoint:** A lesser-known viewpoint with beautiful vistas of Kamala and Surin Beaches.
- **Paradise Beach:** Smaller and less crowded than some other beaches, Paradise Beach is an excellent place to relax and swim.
- **Ao Sane Beach:** A snorkeler's paradise with excellent underwater visibility and diverse marine life. It's less crowded than other popular beaches.
- **Banana Beach:** Accessible by a short boat ride from Bang Tao Beach, Banana Beach offers a quieter and serene escape.
- **Sirinat National Park:** Located near the airport, it's home to beautiful Mai Khao Beach, the longest beach on the island, and a nesting site for sea turtles.
- **Ton Sai Waterfall:** A hidden gem within Khao Phra Thaeo National Park, this waterfall offers a refreshing break from the heat.
- **Kathu Waterfall:** A serene and less-visited waterfall where you can enjoy a nature hike and swim in the pools.
- **Koh Lone:** Also known as "Lonely Island," this less-visited island offers a more peaceful and authentic Thai experience. You can take a short boat ride from Chalong Pier.

Phuket offers a wide variety of experiences, from the lively and bustling to the peaceful and hidden. Whether you're seeking adventure, culture, or relaxation, you can find it on this beautiful island.

Ayutthaya

Ayutthaya, located just north of Bangkok, was once the second capital of the Siamese Kingdom and is now a UNESCO World Heritage Site. It's known for its well-preserved historical ruins and temples, providing a window into Thailand's rich history. Here are some of the tourist highlights, activities, and hidden gems in Ayutthaya:

Tourist Highlights:

- **Ayutthaya Historical Park:** The heart of Ayutthaya's attractions, this park features the remains of temples, palaces, and Buddha statues. Key sites within the park include Wat Phra Si Sanphet, Wat Mahathat (famous for its Buddha head entwined in tree roots), and Wat Ratchaburana.
- **Wat Chaiwatthanaram:** A stunning riverside temple known for its Prang-style architecture and picturesque reflections in the water.
- **Bang Pa-In Royal Palace:** Also known as the Summer Palace, it's a beautiful complex with a mix of architectural styles and landscaped gardens.
- **Elephant Stay:** For a unique experience, you can visit this organization that cares for and offers activities with elephants. It's committed to ethical and responsible elephant tourism.
- **Ayutthaya Floating Market:** Located near Wat Samphao Lom, this market allows you to sample local food, snacks, and souvenirs from vendors on traditional boats along the river.

Tourist Activities:

- **Exploring by Bicycle:** Rent a bicycle and explore the historical sites at your own pace. The flat terrain and small roads make it an ideal way to discover Ayutthaya.
- **Boat Tours:** Take a boat tour along the Chao Phraya River to view the ruins from the water, offering a unique perspective on Ayutthaya's historical sites.
- **Tuk-Tuk Rides:** Consider hiring a tuk-tuk for a fun and convenient way to visit various temples and historical sites.
- **Sunset Viewing:** Watch the sunset from the Chaiwatthanaram temple or one of the riverfront restaurants for a memorable experience.

Hidden Gems:

- **Wat Phu Khao Thong:** This lesser-visited temple offers a serene atmosphere and a viewpoint that provides an excellent panoramic view of Ayutthaya.
- **Wat Phanan Choeng:** Home to a massive, revered Buddha statue, this temple offers a more intimate experience compared to some of the more crowded sites.
- **Wat Yai Chai Mongkhon:** Located just outside the city, this temple features a large reclining Buddha and offers a quieter and more peaceful setting for exploration.
- **Suan Somdet Phra Srinagarindra Park:** A lovely park near the river, perfect for a relaxing stroll or picnic. It's not as well-known, so it tends to be less crowded.

- **Wihan Phramongkhon Bophit:** Home to a gigantic bronze Buddha image, this temple is sometimes overlooked but is worth a visit for its impressive statue.
- **Chao Sam Phraya National Museum:** This museum houses a significant collection of artifacts and art from the Ayutthaya period, providing valuable context for the historical sites you'll visit.

Chiang Rai

Chiang Rai, located in Northern Thailand, is a charming city with a unique blend of cultural and natural attractions. While it may not be as bustling as Bangkok or Chiang Mai, it has its own set of tourist highlights and hidden gems to explore. Here are some of the key attractions and activities:

Tourist Highlights:

- **Wat Rong Khun (White Temple):** Wat Rong Khun is one of Chiang Rai's most famous landmarks. This contemporary Buddhist temple is entirely white, featuring intricate carvings and mirror details. The architecture is otherworldly, and the temple is a masterpiece by Thai artist Chalermchai Kositpipat.
- **Wat Phra Singh:** This temple is one of the most revered in Chiang Rai, featuring stunning Lanna-style architecture, intricate carvings, and a golden chedi (stupa). The temple is known for its serene ambiance and beautiful grounds.
- **Blue Temple (Wat Rong Suea Ten):** The Blue Temple is another contemporary temple in Chiang Rai, known for its striking blue and gold color scheme and intricate

artwork. It's a relatively new attraction but has gained popularity for its unique design.
- **Doi Tung Royal Villa and Mae Fah Luang Garden:** Located in the hills, this former royal residence and garden offer spectacular views and beautiful botanical gardens. You can also visit the Hall of Inspiration, which showcases the life and work of the late Princess Mother, Somdej Phra Srinagarindra.
- **Golden Triangle:** The Golden Triangle, where the borders of Thailand, Myanmar, and Laos meet, is a historically significant area known for its opium trade. Visitors can explore the Opium Museum and enjoy boat trips along the Mekong River.
- **Clock Tower:** Chiang Rai's Clock Tower is an ornate, golden clock tower that comes to life with an enchanting light and sound show in the evenings. It's an iconic landmark and a great spot for photos.

Tourist Activities:

- **Explore Local Markets:** Chiang Rai has several bustling markets like the Night Bazaar and the Saturday Walking Street Market, where you can shop for local handicrafts, clothing, and sample delicious street food.
- **Cycling and Hiking:** The city and its surroundings are great for cycling and hiking. You can explore the countryside, visit local villages, and enjoy the natural beauty of the region.
- **Elephant Sanctuaries:** Chiang Rai is home to ethical elephant sanctuaries where you can observe and interact with elephants in a responsible and sustainable manner.

Hidden Gems:

- **Baan Dam (Black House):** Baan Dam is a unique and somewhat eerie attraction featuring a collection of black-hued buildings and sculptures created by Thai artist Thawan Duchanee. It's a fascinating but lesser-known counterpart to the White Temple.
- **Singha Park:** This expansive park and agricultural farm offer stunning landscapes, a tea plantation, zip-lining, and a range of outdoor activities. It's a great place to relax and enjoy the scenery.
- **Phu Chi Fah:** Located about a 2.5-hour drive from Chiang Rai, Phu Chi Fah is known for its breathtaking sunrise views over the Mekong River and Laos. The viewpoint is best visited in the early morning.

Krabi and Railay Beach

Krabi and Railay Beach are two of Thailand's most beautiful destinations, known for their stunning limestone cliffs, clear waters, and lush landscapes. These areas offer a wide range of tourist activities and hidden gems for visitors to explore:

Krabi:

Tourist Highlights and Activities:

- **Ao Nang Beach:** This is a popular base for travelers in Krabi, known for its beautiful sunsets, vibrant street life, and a variety of restaurants and bars.
- **Railay Beach:** While technically part of Krabi, Railay Beach is often considered a separate destination due to its unique access via boat. The beach is famous for rock climbing, pristine waters, and laid-back vibes.

- **Phra Nang Cave Beach:** Located near Railay, this beach is famous for the Princess Cave (Thung Teao Forest Natural Park) filled with offerings to the spirit of the drowned princess. It's an excellent spot for snorkeling and relaxing.
- **Rock Climbing:** Krabi is one of the world's top rock climbing destinations, with numerous climbing schools and routes for climbers of all levels. Railay is particularly known for its climbing.
- **Island Hopping:** Take boat trips to nearby islands like the Phi Phi Islands and Hong Islands, which offer opportunities for snorkeling and exploring hidden lagoons.
- **Thung Teao Forest Natural Park:** This park is home to the famous Emerald Pool and the Blue Pool, two unique natural attractions where you can take a refreshing dip in clear, emerald-colored water.

Hidden Gems:

- **Ton Sai Beach:** Located near Railay, this beach is quieter and less developed than its famous neighbor, offering a more relaxed atmosphere and lower prices.
- **Hot Springs in Klong Thom:** Located about an hour from Krabi Town, these natural hot springs are a great place to relax in the mineral-rich waters.
- **Tiger Cave Temple (Wat Tham Sua):** A challenging climb to this temple's summit rewards you with panoramic views of the surrounding countryside.
- **Klong Thom Night Market:** Experience local street food and shop for souvenirs in this bustling night market.

Railay Beach:

Tourist Highlights and Activities:

- **Rock Climbing:** Railay is renowned for its world-class rock climbing. Climbers of all levels come here to ascend the iconic limestone karsts.
- **Phra Nang Beach:** The beach is a must-visit, and you can explore the Princess Cave filled with offerings and fertility symbols. Enjoy sunbathing, swimming, and snorkeling.
- **Railay Lagoon:** A hidden gem, the lagoon is accessible by a short hike and offers a serene place for swimming and cliff jumping.
- **Railay Viewpoint:** A moderate hike to the viewpoint provides stunning vistas of the Railay peninsula and its beaches.
- **Mangrove Kayaking:** Paddle through the mangrove forests and explore caves and hidden lagoons with guided kayaking tours.

Hidden Gems:

- **Tonsai Beach:** As mentioned earlier, Tonsai is a less crowded alternative to Railay Beach. It has a relaxed atmosphere, and you can hike to Railay from here during low tide.
- **Phra Nang Cave Beach Secret Lagoon:** Near the Princess Cave on Phra Nang Beach, there's a hidden lagoon accessible through a narrow opening in the rocks.

- **Railay Beach Viewpoint Cave:** A short hike from Railay East Beach takes you to a hidden cave with ancient cave paintings and fantastic views.

Krabi and Railay Beach offer a fantastic combination of adventure, relaxation, and natural beauty. Whether you're into rock climbing, beachcombing, or exploring hidden gems, these destinations have something for every type of traveler.

Sukhothai

A must-visit location for tourists interested in Thailand's history, culture, and ancient ruins is Sukhothai, which is situated in Northern Thailand. Sukhothai is a UNESCO World Heritage Site. The city served as the first capital of the Kingdom of Sukhothai, an important factor in the development of contemporary Thailand. Here are a few of Sukhothai's tourism attractions, events, and undiscovered gems:

Tourist Highlights:

1. **Historical Park of Sukhothai:**
   - The Historical Park of Sukhothai is the primary attraction in the area. It's divided into several zones, with the most significant being the Central Zone. This zone is home to well-preserved ruins, including the Sukhothai Historical Park and Wat Mahathat, which features the iconic seated Buddha image. Exploring the park by bicycle or on foot is a fantastic way to experience the historical ambiance.
2. **Wat Si Sawai:**
   - Located just outside the city walls, Wat Si Sawai is one of the oldest temples in Sukhothai. Its

architecture, characterized by the Khmer-style prangs (towers), showcases the influence of the Khmer Empire.
3. **Wat Saphan Hin:**
   - A climb up to Wat Saphan Hin provides panoramic views of the surrounding countryside. This temple is known for its stone Buddha statue, which is one of the most iconic images of Sukhothai.
4. **Ramkhamhaeng National Museum:**
   - This museum offers an insightful look into the history and culture of Sukhothai through artifacts and historical exhibits. It's an excellent place to gain a deeper understanding of the area's heritage.

Tourist Activities:

1. **Cycling Tours:**
   - Rent a bicycle and explore the historical park and surrounding areas at your own pace. The flat terrain makes it a pleasant and convenient way to see the sights.
2. **Traditional Thai Dance Performances:**
   - Some of the local hotels and cultural centers host traditional Thai dance performances, providing a glimpse into Thai culture and history.
3. **Learn About Ramkhamhaeng's Inscription:**
   - The Ramkhamhaeng Inscription is an essential historical artifact that offers insights into the early Thai script and history. Visit the monument and the nearby museum to learn more about it.
4. **Taste Local Cuisine:**
   - Sukhothai is known for its local dishes, including Sukhothai noodles, which are famous for their

unique flavors. Be sure to sample these regional specialties at local restaurants and street food stalls.

Hidden Gems:

1. **Wat Chang Lom:**
    - Located in the Western Zone of the Historical Park, this temple features a unique elephant-adorned base, which sets it apart from many other Sukhothai temples.
2. **Khao Luang Mountain:**
    - Khao Luang Mountain is a bit of a hidden gem, offering hiking opportunities and beautiful viewpoints. It's a great place to enjoy a tranquil escape from the crowds.
3. **Loy Krathong Festival:**
    - If your visit aligns with the Loy Krathong festival in November, you can experience a magical display of lanterns and floating krathongs (decorated baskets with candles) on the Yom River.
4. **Local Markets:**
    - Explore the local markets to experience everyday life in Sukhothai. The fresh produce and vibrant atmosphere provide a glimpse into the community.

Koh Samui and the Gulf Islands

Koh Samui and the Gulf Islands, located in the Gulf of Thailand, offer a mix of natural beauty, vibrant nightlife, and cultural experiences. Here are some tourist highlights and hidden gems in this region:

Koh Samui:

- **Chaweng Beach:** This is one of the most popular beaches on the island, known for its white sands and clear waters. It's lined with resorts, restaurants, and nightlife options.
- **Lamai Beach:** A slightly quieter alternative to Chaweng, Lamai Beach is famous for the Hin Ta and Hin Yai rocks, natural formations that resemble male and female genitalia.
- **Big Buddha Temple (Wat Phra Yai):** The 12-meter tall golden statue of Buddha is a major landmark on the island. It's located on a small island connected by a causeway.
- **Ang Thong Marine Park:** Take a day trip to this stunning national park, which features emerald lagoons, limestone cliffs, and lush jungles. Activities include snorkeling, hiking, and kayaking.
- **Fisherman's Village:** Located in Bophut, this charming area features historic buildings, boutique shops, and a vibrant night market with street food and entertainment.
- **Namuang Waterfall:** The island's two Namuang Waterfalls offer refreshing swims beneath the cascades and a chance to explore the surrounding forests.

Hidden Gems in Koh Samui:

- **Tarnim Magic Garden:** A hidden sculpture garden created by a local farmer, this spot features stone sculptures, statues, and a serene atmosphere.

- **Secret Buddha Garden:** Located in the hills of Samui, this garden is filled with statues, waterfalls, and lush gardens, and it offers breathtaking views of the island.
- **Hin Lad Waterfall Temple:** A lesser-known temple with a peaceful ambiance. You can hike to the waterfall and explore the temple grounds.

Koh Phangan:

- **Full Moon Party:** The monthly Full Moon Party on Haad Rin Beach is legendary for its beachfront dance music festival that draws revelers from around the world.
- **Haad Yao Beach:** This beautiful, serene beach is perfect for relaxation and water sports.
- **Thong Sala Night Market:** A vibrant night market where you can sample local street food and shop for souvenirs.
- **Than Sadet Waterfall:** Located in a national park, this waterfall is considered sacred and was often visited by Thai kings.

Hidden Gems in Koh Phangan:

- **Bottle Beach:** Accessible only by boat or a challenging hike, this tranquil beach offers peace and seclusion.
- **Haad Salad:** A beautiful and quiet beach destination known for its stunning sunsets and great snorkeling opportunities.

Koh Tao:

- **Scuba Diving:** Koh Tao is renowned for its affordable scuba diving certification courses and vibrant marine life, making it a top destination for divers.
- **Sairee Beach:** The main beach on the island, Sairee Beach is lined with bars, restaurants, and shops.
- **John-Suwan Viewpoint:** Hike to this viewpoint for panoramic vistas of the island and the surrounding seas.

Hidden Gems in Koh Tao:

- **Shark Island:** This tiny islet near Koh Tao is excellent for snorkeling and is home to a variety of marine life, including reef sharks.
- **Mango Viewpoint:** Offering fantastic views, this viewpoint is less crowded than John-Suwan, providing a more peaceful experience.

Pattaya

Pattaya is a coastal city in Thailand known for its lively nightlife, beautiful beaches, and a wide range of tourist activities. Here are some of the tourist highlights and hidden gems in Pattaya:

Tourist Highlights:

- **Pattaya Beach:** The city's main beach, Pattaya Beach, offers a wide array of water sports, including jet skiing, parasailing, and banana boat rides. The beach promenade is lined with restaurants, bars, and shops.

- **Walking Street:** Pattaya's most famous nightlife district, Walking Street, comes alive in the evenings. It's known for its bars, nightclubs, and a vibrant atmosphere. This is where you can experience Pattaya's renowned nightlife.
- **Sanctuary of Truth:** This stunning, hand-carved wooden temple is a unique attraction in Pattaya. It's a fusion of Thai, Khmer, Chinese, and Hindu architectural styles, and it's set against the backdrop of the sea.
- **Nong Nooch Tropical Botanical Garden:** Located a short drive from Pattaya, this sprawling garden features beautifully landscaped grounds, cultural shows, and themed gardens. It's a serene escape from the hustle and bustle of the city.
- **Coral Island (Koh Larn):** Take a short boat ride to Coral Island to enjoy clear waters, snorkeling, and water sports. The island is known for its pristine beaches and vibrant marine life.
- **Art in Paradise:** This interactive 3D art museum is a fun and family-friendly attraction. Visitors can pose with the optical illusions created by the artworks for some memorable photos.

Hidden Gems:

- **Koh Samae San:** This tranquil island is located within the Royal Thai Navy base, making it less crowded than other islands near Pattaya. It's a fantastic spot for snorkeling and relaxation. Be sure to obtain permission to visit.
- **The Million Years Stone Park & Crocodile Farm:** This unique park features rock gardens, exotic plants, and a

crocodile farm. You can watch thrilling crocodile shows and see impressive stone sculptures.
- **Wat Yansangwararam:** This serene and less-visited temple complex offers impressive architecture and beautiful gardens. The nearby Khao Chi Chan Buddha, a giant carved image on a mountain, is also worth a visit.
- **Silverlake Vineyard:** Located outside Pattaya, this vineyard offers picturesque vineyards, Mediterranean-inspired architecture, and a lovely restaurant with vineyard views. It's an unexpected find in a coastal city.
- **Khao Phra Tamnak:** This hill offers panoramic views of Pattaya Bay, Jomtien Beach, and the islands. It's a quieter spot compared to some of the busier viewpoints.
- **Wat Tham Yai Prik:** Located in the countryside, this temple features impressive caves and intricate rock carvings, and it's an excellent place to explore away from the city center.
- **Mini Siam:** A miniature park displaying replicas of famous landmarks from around the world. It's a quirky but fascinating attraction for those interested in scale models.
- **Kao Chee Chan:** This large Buddha image carved into a cliffside is often overlooked by tourists. It's an excellent place for reflection and photography.

Kanchanaburi

Kanchanaburi, a province in western Thailand, is a region known for its historical significance and stunning natural beauty. It offers a range of tourist highlights, activities, and hidden gems that cater to both history enthusiasts and nature lovers. Here are some of the top attractions and lesser-known gems in Kanchanaburi:

Tourist Highlights:

- **Death Railway (Burma Railway):** The Death Railway, constructed during World War II, is a major historical site in Kanchanaburi. Visitors can explore the infamous Hellfire Pass and take a ride on the scenic train that runs along the railway, offering breathtaking views of the River Kwai and surrounding landscapes.
- **Erawan National Park:** Erawan National Park is home to the famous Erawan Falls, a series of emerald green ponds and cascading waterfalls. The park offers hiking trails, swimming opportunities, and the chance to explore the seven tiers of the falls.
- **Kanchanaburi War Cemetery:** Pay your respects at the Kanchanaburi War Cemetery, the final resting place for thousands of Allied prisoners of war who lost their lives during the construction of the Death Railway.
- **Bridge Over the River Kwai:** The historical bridge is an iconic landmark in Kanchanaburi. Visitors can walk across the bridge, visit the museum, and learn more about its World War II history.
- **Lawa Cave:** Located within Erawan National Park, Lawa Cave is a hidden gem. Explore this unique limestone cave, which features beautiful stalactites and stalagmites.

Tourist Activities:

- **Elephant World:** A sanctuary for retired and rescued elephants, Elephant World offers visitors the opportunity to interact with and care for these majestic animals in an ethical and responsible manner.
- **Rock Climbing in Nam Tok:** The Nam Tok area near Kanchanaburi offers excellent rock climbing opportunities for enthusiasts of all skill levels. There are several climbing schools and tour operators in the region.
- **Mon Bridge:** Visit the Mon Bridge, one of the longest wooden bridges in Thailand. This area offers an authentic glimpse into the lives of the Mon people, known for their unique culture and traditions.
- **Tham Than Lot National Park:** This national park features a series of caves and caverns. The highlight is the Tham Than Lot Noi Cave, where you can take a boat ride through the stunning cave system.

Hidden Gems:

- **Lum Sum Waterfall:** Located in a serene and less-visited area of Erawan National Park, Lum Sum Waterfall is a hidden gem that's worth the extra effort to reach.
- **Wat Tham Sua (Tiger Cave Temple):** Although not widely known, this temple offers breathtaking panoramic views of the surrounding countryside from a hilltop. The temple is also known for its caves and meditation spots.
- **Phra Thaen Cave Temple:** Explore this unique temple, which is set within a limestone cave complex. It's an

intriguing blend of religion and nature, with Buddha statues and shrines within the cave.
- **Kanchanaburi Night Market:** While not entirely hidden, the Kanchanaburi Night Market offers a delightful local experience with street food, live music, and a vibrant atmosphere.

Koh Phi Phi

Koh Phi Phi, part of the Phi Phi Islands in the Andaman Sea, is one of Thailand's most popular and picturesque destinations. It's known for its stunning natural beauty, vibrant nightlife, and a wide range of activities for tourists. Here are some of the tourist highlights and hidden gems on Koh Phi Phi:

Tourist Highlights:

- **Phi Phi Viewpoint (Phi Phi Don):** Hike up to this viewpoint for a panoramic view of the twin bays and the famous natural indentation that separates them, known as the "Hin Kho Beach."
- **Maya Bay (Phi Phi Leh):** Although closed for environmental restoration at the time of my knowledge cutoff in September 2021, Maya Bay is a stunning location featured in the movie "The Beach." Visitors can still view the bay from a distance or enjoy nearby snorkeling sites.
- **Long Beach (Phi Phi Don):** Relax on the long stretch of golden sand and swim in the clear waters. It's a great spot for sunbathing and water sports.

- **Monkey Beach (Phi Phi Don):** Visit this unique beach where you can see playful monkeys. Be cautious and do not feed them, as they can be aggressive.
- **Snorkeling and Diving:** Koh Phi Phi offers fantastic underwater experiences. Snorkel at locations like Shark Point and Bamboo Island, or go diving to explore colorful coral reefs and marine life.
- **Nightlife in Tonsai Village:** Tonsai Village on Phi Phi Don comes alive at night with an array of bars, nightclubs, and fire shows. Enjoy beachfront parties and a vibrant nightlife scene.

Tourist Activities:

- **Island-Hopping Tours:** Join boat tours to explore nearby islands, such as Bamboo Island, Mosquito Island, and Bamboo Island. Many tours include snorkeling and swimming stops.
- **Kayaking:** Rent a kayak to explore the stunning limestone cliffs and hidden coves surrounding the islands.
- **Rock Climbing:** Koh Phi Phi's towering limestone cliffs make it a popular destination for rock climbing. Many operators offer climbing courses for all skill levels.
- **Thai Cooking Classes:** Learn to prepare delicious Thai dishes during a cooking class. Enjoy your culinary creations afterward.

Hidden Gems:

- **Bida Nok and Bida Nai:** These two dive sites near Koh Phi Phi Leh are less crowded than some other sites.

They are known for their diverse marine life and underwater landscapes.
- **Phi Phi Reggae Bar:** Located on Phi Phi Don, this bar offers nightly fire shows and an energetic atmosphere. Try their signature "Reggae Buckets."
- **Loh Moo Dee Beach (Phi Phi Leh):** A quieter alternative to Maya Bay, this secluded beach offers beautiful surroundings and excellent snorkeling opportunities.
- **Loh Lana Bay:** A hidden gem on Phi Phi Don, this small bay is perfect for a peaceful escape. It's accessible by boat or a short hike.
- **Laem Tong Beach (Phi Phi Don):** A serene and less-visited beach on the northern tip of Phi Phi Don. It's home to some upscale resorts and offers a peaceful ambiance.
- **Sunset at Ao Tonsai:** While the nightlife gets going after dark, watching the sunset at Ao Tonsai (Tonsai Bay) can be a serene and beautiful experience.

The Chumphon Archipelago

The Chumphon Archipelago, situated in the Gulf of Thailand, is a lesser-known gem with pristine natural beauty, diverse marine life, and tranquil island experiences. Comprising several islands, including Koh Tao, Koh Samui, Koh Phangan, and Koh Nang Yuan, this region offers a range of activities for tourists. Here are the tourist highlights and some hidden gems in the Chumphon Archipelago:

Koh Tao:

- **Diving and Snorkeling:** Koh Tao is renowned for its excellent scuba diving and snorkeling sites. Crystal-clear waters, colorful coral reefs, and abundant marine life make it a diver's paradise. Shark Island, Sail Rock, and Japanese Gardens are popular dive sites.
- **Sairee Beach:** Sairee Beach is the main beach on Koh Tao, lined with restaurants, bars, and shops. It's a great place to relax, enjoy sunsets, and engage in water sports.
- **Viewpoints:** Hike to John-Suwan Viewpoint and Love Koh Tao Viewpoint for panoramic views of the island.
- **Hidden Gem: Mango Viewpoint:** For a quieter experience, visit Mango Viewpoint, where you can admire the scenic surroundings in relative solitude.
- **Rock Climbing:** Koh Tao offers excellent rock climbing opportunities, especially at the climbing spots on the western side of the island.

Koh Samui:

- **Chaweng Beach:** The most popular and developed beach on Koh Samui, offering a wide range of accommodations, restaurants, and nightlife.
- **Big Buddha Temple (Wat Phra Yai):** Visit the iconic Big Buddha statue, an important religious site.
- **Ang Thong Marine Park:** Take a day trip to this stunning archipelago, known for its emerald lagoon, limestone cliffs, and lush jungle. Activities include hiking, snorkeling, and kayaking.
- **Fisherman's Village:** Located in Bophut, this charming area is known for its Friday Night Walking Street

Market, featuring street food, shopping, and live entertainment.
- **Hidden Gem: Secret Buddha Garden (Tarnim Magic Garden):** Tucked away in the hills, this garden showcases a collection of statues and sculptures in a serene, lush setting.

Koh Phangan:

- **Full Moon Party:** Koh Phangan is famous for its Full Moon Party, a lively and colorful beach festival that takes place every month on Haad Rin Beach.
- **Haad Rin:** While known for the Full Moon Party, Haad Rin is a beautiful beach to visit during the day, with excellent swimming and water sports.
- **Wat Phu Khao Noi:** Visit this hilltop temple for stunning views of the island and the sea.
- **Hidden Gem: Secret Beaches:** Explore some of the less crowded beaches on the island, such as Haad Thian and Haad Yao, for a more peaceful experience.

Koh Nang Yuan:

- **Island Hopping:** Koh Nang Yuan is a short boat ride from Koh Tao and is famous for its three small, interconnected islands. Hike up to the viewpoint for a breathtaking panoramic view.
- **Snorkeling:** The waters around Koh Nang Yuan are excellent for snorkeling, with vibrant coral reefs and marine life.
- **Hidden Gem: Early Arrival:** To avoid the crowds, try to arrive early in the morning before the day-trippers from nearby islands arrive.

Nakhon Pathom

Nakhon Pathom is a historic city located just 56 kilometers west of Bangkok and is home to several significant tourist highlights, including the world's tallest stupa, rich cultural heritage, and various hidden gems. Here are the main tourist highlights and activities in Nakhon Pathom:

1. Phra Pathom Chedi:

- The most iconic attraction in Nakhon Pathom is the Phra Pathom Chedi, also known as the Great Stupa. This stupa is the world's tallest stupa, standing at an impressive 127 meters. It's a significant Buddhist pilgrimage site and a breathtaking architectural wonder. You can climb to the top for panoramic views of the surrounding area.

2. Sanam Chandra Palace:

- This beautiful palace complex is located near Phra Pathom Chedi and is surrounded by lush gardens and a lake. It was once the summer residence of King Rama VI. The palace and its grounds are open to the public and offer a glimpse into the life of Thai royalty.

3. Wat Phra Prathon Chedi:

- Located near the Great Stupa, this temple is home to a massive golden chedi. It's a serene and less crowded spot where you can explore the temple grounds and enjoy some quiet moments.

4. Nakhon Pathom Cultural Center:

- This center showcases the history and culture of Nakhon Pathom through exhibits and artifacts. It's an excellent place to learn more about the local heritage.

5. Wat Rai Khing:

- Located a bit outside of the city, this temple is known for its picturesque architecture, including a white stupa and a reclining Buddha statue.

6. Hidden Gems and Local Activities:

- **Don Wai Floating Market:** Located on the banks of the Tha Chin River, this charming floating market offers a wide range of street food, fresh produce, and local crafts. It's less touristy than some of the floating markets in Bangkok.
- **Ban Khu Bua Ancient City:** A historical park with ancient ruins and sculptures, some dating back over 1,000 years. It's a lesser-known site with an air of tranquility.
- **Nakhon Pathom Local Markets:** Explore local markets in the city to sample authentic Thai dishes and shop for traditional handicrafts. Try the local specialties like Khanom Jeen (rice noodles) and fresh fruits.
- **Thung Khwang Floating Market:** Another lesser-known floating market in Nakhon Pathom, it's a great place to experience a more relaxed and local atmosphere while enjoying a variety of Thai snacks and dishes.

- **Ban Pong Canals:** Take a boat ride along the serene canals of Ban Pong to discover the rural way of life and picturesque scenery.
- **Kao Mhong Mountain and Royal Thai Air Force Academy Museum:** This area offers hiking opportunities, and the museum showcases the history of the Royal Thai Air Force.

Prachuap Khiri Khan

Prachuap Khiri Khan is a picturesque province in Thailand, located along the Gulf of Thailand, about 230 kilometers southwest of Bangkok. It's known for its natural beauty, charming town of Hua Hin, and nearby hidden gems. Here are the tourist highlights and activities in Prachuap Khiri Khan:

1. Hua Hin Beach:

- Hua Hin's long and sandy beach is the main attraction for many visitors. You can relax on the beach, swim in the calm waters, and enjoy beachside activities such as horseback riding.

2. Hua Hin Night Market:

- This bustling market is a great place to experience the local atmosphere and indulge in delicious street food. You'll find various stalls selling everything from fresh seafood to handicrafts and clothing.

3. Phra Mahathat Chedi Pakdee Prakas:

- This hilltop temple offers panoramic views of Hua Hin and the Gulf of Thailand. It's also known for its 17-meter high golden Buddha statue.

4. Wat Khao Takiap (Monkey Temple):

- This temple, located on Monkey Mountain, is home to a large troop of monkeys. You can climb the stairs to the temple and enjoy stunning views of the coastline.

5. Khao Sam Roi Yot National Park:

- Located about an hour south of Hua Hin, this national park features limestone formations, caves, and wetlands. One of its highlights is Phraya Nakhon Cave, home to a beautiful pavilion known as Kuha Karuhas Pavilion, which is illuminated by a hole in the cave roof.

6. Dolphin Watching:

- Take a boat tour from Pranburi or Sam Roi Yot to spot the local Irrawaddy dolphins in the Gulf of Thailand.

Hidden Gems:

7. Huay Yang Waterfall:

- Located around 60 kilometers south of Hua Hin, this serene waterfall is nestled in a lush forest. It's a great place for a refreshing swim and a picnic.

8. Kuiburi National Park:

- This national park is famous for its wildlife, particularly the herds of wild elephants that can be observed on guided tours. It's an off-the-beaten-path gem for nature lovers.

9. Ao Manao Beach:

- A little further south of Prachuap Khiri Khan town is this picturesque bay with a lovely beach and clear waters. It's an ideal spot for swimming and relaxation.

10. Wat Ao Noi (Wat Tham Khao Tao): - Located in a cave by the sea, this temple is a hidden gem known for its tranquil and unique location. You can visit the temple and enjoy the scenic surroundings.

11. Sam Roi Yot Fishing Village: - Explore this traditional fishing village to witness the daily life of local fishermen, see colorful fishing boats, and enjoy fresh seafood at the local restaurants.

Pai

Pai is a charming town located in the mountains of Northern Thailand, known for its relaxed atmosphere, stunning natural beauty, and unique cultural experiences. It has become a popular destination for backpackers and travelers seeking a serene retreat. Here are some of the tourist highlights, activities, and hidden gems in Pai:

Tourist Highlights:

- **Pai Canyon (Kong Lan):** Also known as the Grand Canyon of Pai, this natural wonder offers breathtaking views of the surrounding landscape. Visitors can hike along narrow ridges and explore the numerous viewpoints.
- **Pai Walking Street:** Like many Thai towns, Pai has its own vibrant night market. The Pai Walking Street comes alive in the evenings, offering a wide range of street food, local crafts, and live music.
- **Pai Hot Springs:** Relax in the natural hot springs located just a short drive from town. The springs are divided into different pools with varying temperatures, allowing you to soak in the warm mineral-rich waters.
- **Pai World War II Memorial Bridge:** This historic bridge was constructed during World War II and is a reminder of the region's past. It's a peaceful spot to explore and learn about the area's history.
- **Wat Phra That Mae Yen:** Perched on a hill, this temple offers panoramic views of Pai and the surrounding mountains. The highlight is a white Buddha statue that can be seen from various points in the town.

Tourist Activities:

- **Motorbike Tours:** Rent a scooter or motorbike and explore the scenic countryside surrounding Pai. Drive along winding mountain roads, visit waterfalls, and discover hidden villages.
- **Waterfalls:** Pai is home to several stunning waterfalls, including Pam Bok Waterfall, Mor Paeng Waterfall,

and Mo Paeng Waterfall. These natural wonders are perfect for swimming and picnicking.
- **Yun Lai Viewpoint:** A short hike leads to Yun Lai Viewpoint, where you can take in panoramic vistas of the Pai Valley and surrounding mountains. The viewpoint is especially popular for sunrise and sunset.
- **Trekking:** Join a guided trekking tour to explore the lush hills and hill tribe villages around Pai. These tours often provide insight into the culture and traditions of the local communities.
- **Cafes and Chill-Out Spots:** Pai is known for its laid-back atmosphere, and there are numerous cozy cafes and chill-out spots where you can relax, read a book, or enjoy a cup of coffee.

Hidden Gems:

- **Land Split:** This unique geological phenomenon, the "Land Split," offers a glimpse of how the earth cracked during an earthquake. The owner of the property has set up a delightful fruit and snack stand where you can sample local produce and enjoy a fresh fruit shake.
- **Pai Bamboo Bridge:** Located in the Pai countryside, this bamboo bridge provides a peaceful stroll through rice fields and offers lovely views. The entrance fee supports the local community.
- **Tha Pai World War II Memorial Bridge:** Often overshadowed by the more famous Pai Memorial Bridge, this one is quieter and less crowded, offering a tranquil spot to reflect on history.
- **Sai Ngam Hot Spring:** This natural hot spring is less known to tourists, making it a peaceful and relaxing

place to soak in the thermal waters surrounded by lush forest.
- **Cafes off the Beaten Path:** Pai is filled with quaint cafes, some of which are hidden in the countryside. Explore the backroads to discover charming spots with serene views and excellent coffee.

Pai's laid-back atmosphere, beautiful natural surroundings, and unique cultural experiences make it a special destination in Thailand. While the tourist highlights are well-known, the hidden gems and off-the-beaten-path activities provide a more intimate and authentic glimpse of the area.

Chapter 3: Itineraries

1. **Efficient Use of Time:** An itinerary helps you make the most of your limited time in Thailand. It ensures you have a plan for each day and can fit in the attractions and experiences that matter most to you.
2. **Prioritization:** Thailand is a diverse country with a wide range of things to see and do. An itinerary allows you to prioritize the activities and places you're most interested in, helping you avoid missing out on must-see attractions.
3. **Budget Planning:** Planning your activities in advance can help you budget for your trip more effectively. It allows you to estimate costs, including accommodation, transportation, and entrance fees.
4. **Logistics:** Thailand is a large country with varying climates and landscapes. Planning your itinerary helps you navigate the logistics of traveling between cities, islands, and regions, ensuring you have a smooth and stress-free journey.

5. **Availability:** Certain attractions, tours, and accommodations may have limited availability, especially during peak travel seasons. Having an itinerary helps you book popular activities and secure the best accommodations in advance.
6. **Cultural Understanding:** Thailand has a rich cultural heritage, and understanding the local customs, festivals, and holidays can enhance your travel experience. An itinerary can incorporate opportunities to participate in cultural events and activities.
7. **Adventure and Exploration:** While planning your itinerary, you can discover off-the-beaten-path destinations and hidden gems that you might not have known about otherwise, enriching your travel experience.
8. **Safety:** An itinerary can also help you consider safety factors. For instance, knowing the current weather conditions and potential risks in specific areas can help you make informed decisions about your travel plans.
9. **Memorable Experiences:** Thailand offers a wide range of experiences, from relaxing on pristine beaches to exploring ancient temples and lively markets. An itinerary allows you to craft a trip that offers a balanced mix of these experiences, creating unforgettable memories.
10. **Flexibility:** While it's important to have a plan, your itinerary doesn't have to be rigid. It can be a flexible guide that you can adjust as you go, based on personal preferences, local recommendations, and unforeseen circumstances. It's there to help you, not restrict you.

One week Itinerary

Day 1: Arrival in Bangkok

- Arrive at Suvarnabhumi Airport in Bangkok.
- Check into your accommodation.
- Explore the local area, sample street food, and get a taste of Bangkok's bustling street life.

Day 2: Bangkok - Grand Palace and Wat Pho

- Visit the Grand Palace, a stunning complex of temples and royal buildings.
- Explore Wat Pho, known for the giant Reclining Buddha.
- Stroll through the nearby streets and sample more Thai street food.
- In the evening, consider a visit to Asiatique the Riverfront, a night market and entertainment complex.

Day 3: Bangkok - Canal Tour and Temples

- Take a traditional Thai longtail boat tour along the canals (klongs) to see a different side of Bangkok.
- Visit Wat Arun, the Temple of Dawn, and Wat Saket (the Golden Mount).
- Explore the vibrant neighborhood of Khao San Road.

Day 4: Ayutthaya Day Trip

- Depart for Ayutthaya, an ancient city just north of Bangkok.

- Explore the Ayutthaya Historical Park, home to the ruins of temples and palaces from the Ayutthaya Kingdom.
- Return to Bangkok in the evening.

Day 5: Chiang Mai

- Fly to Chiang Mai, a city in Northern Thailand.
- Check into your accommodation.
- Explore the Old City of Chiang Mai and visit the Wat Phra Singh temple.

Day 6: Chiang Mai - Doi Suthep and Hill Tribes

- Visit Wat Phra That Doi Suthep, a beautiful hilltop temple with panoramic views.
- Join a guided tour to visit hill tribe villages and learn about their unique cultures.
- Explore Chiang Mai's night bazaars and markets for souvenirs and local crafts.

Day 7: Chiang Mai - Elephant Sanctuary and Departure

- Spend your morning at an ethical elephant sanctuary, where you can interact with rescued elephants and learn about their conservation.
- In the afternoon, return to Chiang Mai and catch your flight back to Bangkok.
- Depending on your flight schedule, you might have time for some last-minute shopping or sightseeing in Bangkok before your departure.

Two weeks Itinerary

Day 1-3: Bangkok

- **Day 1:**
  - Arrival in Bangkok, check-in to your accommodation.
  - Visit the Grand Palace, Wat Pho, and Wat Arun.
  - Explore the bustling street markets like Khao San Road in the evening.
- **Day 2:**
  - Take a boat ride along the Chao Phraya River.
  - Explore Jim Thompson House and Erawan Shrine.
  - Enjoy nightlife in Bangkok's entertainment districts.
- **Day 3:**
  - Visit Chatuchak Weekend Market (if visiting on a weekend).
  - Explore local markets and street food.
  - Depart for Ayutthaya in the afternoon.

Day 4: Ayutthaya

- Spend the day exploring the historical city of Ayutthaya, a UNESCO World Heritage Site.
- Visit temples and ancient ruins, such as Wat Mahathat and Wat Ratchaburana.
- Return to Bangkok in the evening.

Day 5-7: Chiang Mai

- **Day 5:**
  - Fly to Chiang Mai.
  - Visit Wat Phra Singh and explore the Old City.

- Evening visit to the Night Bazaar.
- **Day 6:**
  - Explore Doi Suthep Temple and enjoy panoramic views of Chiang Mai.
  - Visit local markets, such as Warorot Market.
  - Take part in a traditional Thai cooking class.
- **Day 7:**
  - Visit an elephant sanctuary for an ethical elephant experience.
  - Explore the Karen Long Neck Village (optional).
  - Spend the evening at the lively Chiang Mai Night Safari.

Day 8-10: Pai

- **Day 8:**
  - Drive to Pai (approximately 3-4 hours from Chiang Mai).
  - Visit Pai Canyon and enjoy the sunset views.
  - Explore the Pai Walking Street at night.
- **Day 9:**
  - Explore the hot springs and waterfalls in and around Pai.
  - Take a motorbike ride to the Land Split, Pai Bamboo Bridge, and more.
- **Day 10:**
  - Relax and explore more of Pai.
  - Consider a visit to the surrounding hill tribe villages.
  - Drive back to Chiang Mai in the evening.

Day 11-14: Southern Thailand Beaches

- **Day 11:**
    - Fly to Phuket.
    - Visit Patong Beach and the vibrant nightlife.
- **Day 12-13:**
    - Explore the beautiful beaches and islands of the Phuket region, including Phi Phi Islands, James Bond Island, and more.
    - Enjoy water sports, snorkeling, and relaxation.
- **Day 14:**
    - Return to Phuket, explore the town, and do some last-minute shopping.
    - Depart for your home country.

Chapter 4:
Best Restaurants and Cuisine

Thai cuisine is renowned worldwide for its bold and vibrant flavors, combining sweet, salty, sour, and spicy elements to create dishes that tantalize the taste buds. The cuisine is incredibly diverse, with regional variations and a wide range of ingredients. Here's an overview of Thai cuisine:

Key Features of Thai Cuisine:

1. **Balanced Flavors:** Thai cuisine is renowned for achieving a perfect balance of flavors in each dish. Sweetness often comes from ingredients like palm sugar, fruit, or sweet sauces. Saltiness is derived from fish sauce or soy sauce. Sourness is achieved through lime or tamarind juice, and spiciness is imparted by chili peppers. The combination of these four tastes creates a harmonious and complex flavor profile.

2. **Rice as a Staple:** Rice is the dietary staple in Thailand and accompanies almost every meal. The most common variety is fragrant Jasmine rice, but in northern and northeastern regions, glutinous or sticky rice is prevalent and is often eaten with the hands.
3. **Herbs and Spices:** Thai cuisine uses a wide array of fresh herbs and spices to create distinctive flavors. Lemongrass, galangal (similar to ginger), kaffir lime leaves, cilantro, basil, and chili peppers are key ingredients. These fresh herbs and spices contribute to the aromatic quality of Thai dishes.
4. **Coconut Milk:** Coconut milk is a fundamental ingredient in many Thai dishes, especially curries and soups. It adds creaminess and a mild sweetness to the dishes while balancing the heat of spices.
5. **Fish Sauce (Nam Pla):** Fish sauce is a key element in Thai cuisine, providing a deep umami flavor and saltiness. It is used in many dishes to season and enhance their taste.
6. **Street Food Culture:** Thailand is famous for its vibrant street food culture. Street vendors offer a variety of affordable and delicious dishes, making it a convenient way to experience authentic Thai cuisine. Whether you're in bustling Bangkok or a quiet rural town, you'll find street food vendors serving up local favorites.

Popular Thai Dishes:

1. **Pad Thai:** This internationally recognized dish is a stir-fried noodle dish made with rice noodles, eggs, tofu or shrimp, and flavored with a tamarind-based sauce. It's garnished with crushed peanuts, lime wedges, and chili flakes.

2. **Tom Yum:** Tom Yum is a spicy and sour soup that's typically made with shrimp or chicken. The soup base includes ingredients like lemongrass, kaffir lime leaves, galangal, and chili peppers.
3. **Green Curry (Kaeng Khiao Wan):** This aromatic and spicy curry is made with green chili paste, coconut milk, and a choice of meat or vegetables. It's known for its vibrant green color.
4. **Massaman Curry:** Massaman curry is a milder and sweeter curry with Muslim influences, featuring meat (often beef), potatoes, and peanuts.
5. **Som Tum (Papaya Salad):** This refreshing salad is made with shredded green papaya, lime juice, fish sauce, and chilies. It can be customized with different levels of spiciness.
6. **Phad Krapow:** A popular stir-fry dish featuring basil leaves, chili, garlic, and a choice of protein (commonly pork, chicken, or seafood). It's often served with rice and a fried egg.
7. **Mango Sticky Rice (Khao Niew Mamuang):** This beloved Thai dessert consists of ripe mangoes, glutinous rice, and a drizzling of sweet coconut milk.
8. **Tom Kha Gai:** Tom Kha Gai is a creamy and aromatic soup made with chicken, coconut milk, and a mix of herbs and spices. It has a distinct coconut and lemongrass flavor.
9. **Gai Pad Med Mamuang:** A stir-fry dish made with chicken, cashew nuts, and a savory sauce. It's often cooked with vegetables and served with rice.
10. **Grilled Satay (Satay Gai):** Satay consists of skewers of marinated and grilled meat, typically chicken or pork. They are served with a flavorful peanut sauce and a cucumber-onion relish.

Regional Variations:

- **Northern Thai Cuisine (Lanna):** This region is known for dishes such as khao soi (a coconut curry noodle soup), sai ua (a flavorful spicy sausage), and kanom jeen nam ngiaw (a noodle soup with a tomato-based broth).
- **Northeastern Thai Cuisine (Isan):** Isan cuisine is famous for its extensive use of sticky rice, som tam (spicy papaya salad), larb (spicy minced meat salad), and grilled meats.
- **Southern Thai Cuisine:** Southern Thai dishes are spicier than those from other regions. They include dishes like massaman curry, green curry, and gaeng som (a tangy curry).
- **Central Thai Cuisine:** The central region, including Bangkok, is known for its diverse street food offerings. Pad Thai, tom yum, and green curry are popular dishes.

Vegetarian and Vegan Options: Thai cuisine is accommodating to vegetarians and vegans, with many meat-free options available. You can enjoy dishes like green curry with tofu, vegetable pad Thai, and a variety of vegetable soups and stir-fries.

Overall, Thai cuisine is a delightful fusion of flavors and ingredients that reflects the country's rich history and cultural diversity. It's a culinary experience that caters to a wide range of tastes, from mild and sweet to fiery and spicy, and it's an essential part of any visit to Thailand.

Restaurants

Here are some top restaurants in various parts of Thailand that visitors should consider for a memorable dining experience:

1. Gaggan (Bangkok):

- Located in Bangkok, Gaggan is a Michelin-starred restaurant known for its innovative and avant-garde approach to Indian cuisine. The chef, Gaggan Anand, has earned international acclaim for his tasting menu, which explores the world of molecular gastronomy.

2. Nahm (Bangkok):

- Another Michelin-starred restaurant in Bangkok, Nahm is famous for its authentic and elevated Thai cuisine. Chef Pim Techamuanvivit offers a sophisticated menu featuring traditional Thai flavors and regional specialties.

3. Issaya Siamese Club (Bangkok):

- Set in a charming colonial villa, this restaurant combines traditional Thai dishes with modern twists. The lush garden setting adds to the delightful dining experience.

4. Bo.Lan (Bangkok):

- Bo.Lan is dedicated to showcasing traditional Thai recipes using locally sourced, organic ingredients. It's known for its commitment to sustainability and offers both à la carte and set menu options.

5. Le Du (Bangkok):

- Le Du is a Michelin-starred restaurant that offers modern Thai cuisine with a focus on local and seasonal ingredients. Chef Thitid "Ton" Tassanakajohn combines traditional flavors with contemporary techniques.

6. Suay (Chiang Mai):

- Suay in Chiang Mai offers a unique blend of Thai and European cuisine. The restaurant is known for its innovative dishes, relaxed atmosphere, and a wide selection of wines.

7. David's Kitchen (Chiang Mai):

- Located in a beautiful villa, David's Kitchen is a French-Thai restaurant that serves delectable fusion cuisine. The restaurant is known for its romantic ambiance and excellent wine selection.

8. Acqua (Phuket):

- Acqua in Phuket offers a contemporary Italian dining experience. The restaurant features a stunning view of Patong Bay and is known for its seafood dishes and homemade pasta.

9. Blue Elephant (Phuket):

- Set in a beautifully restored colonial mansion, Blue Elephant is renowned for its traditional Thai cuisine. It offers a cooking school where visitors can learn to make their favorite Thai dishes.

10. Nahmyaa (Koh Samui): - Located at the Iniala Beach House in Koh Samui, Nahmyaa is known for its southern Thai cuisine. It offers a relaxed beachfront setting and an extensive menu of classic Thai dishes.

11. Rock Salt (Krabi): - Perched on a cliff overlooking Tubkaek Beach in Krabi, Rock Salt offers a delightful dining experience with an extensive seafood menu and breathtaking views.

Chapter 5: Accommodations in Thailand

Thailand offers a wide range of accommodation options to suit the preferences and budgets of all types of visitors. Whether you're looking for luxury resorts, boutique hotels, budget hostels, or unique stays, Thailand has something for everyone. Here are some common accommodation options for visitors:

1. Hotels:

- **Luxury Hotels:** Thailand is home to many world-class luxury hotels and resorts, particularly in popular tourist destinations like Bangkok, Phuket, and Chiang Mai. These accommodations often offer stunning views, exceptional service, and a wide range of amenities.

- **Boutique Hotels:** Boutique hotels provide a more intimate and personalized experience. They often feature unique design, character, and local charm.
- **Mid-Range Hotels:** There are plenty of mid-range hotels with comfortable rooms, modern amenities, and competitive prices.
- **Budget Hotels:** Budget travelers can find affordable hotels in most areas of Thailand. While the amenities may be basic, these options provide clean and comfortable accommodation.
- **Airport Hotels:** If you have a late arrival or early departure, airport hotels are convenient options near major airports like Suvarnabhumi Airport in Bangkok.

2. Hostels:

- Hostels are popular among budget travelers and backpackers. They offer dormitory-style rooms with shared facilities, as well as private rooms in some cases. Hostels are excellent places to meet fellow travelers and often have social common areas.

3. Guesthouses:

- Guesthouses are small, family-run accommodations that can be found throughout Thailand. They often provide a cozy and homely atmosphere. You can find guesthouses in various price ranges.

4. Resorts:

- Thailand is known for its beautiful beach resorts, particularly in places like Phuket, Krabi, and Koh Samui. These beachfront resorts offer stunning sea views, swimming pools, spa facilities, and various water sports.

5. Villas and Vacation Rentals:

- Many visitors opt to rent private villas or vacation homes, especially for longer stays or group trips. These rentals often come with fully equipped kitchens, spacious living areas, and private pools.

6. Backpacker and Diving Lodges:

- In destinations like Koh Tao, which is renowned for scuba diving, you'll find dive lodges and budget accommodations geared toward diving enthusiasts.

7. Homestays:

- Homestays offer a unique opportunity to immerse yourself in Thai culture by staying with a local family. You can find homestays in rural and less touristy areas.

8. Floating Bungalows:

- In regions like Khao Sok National Park, visitors can stay in floating bungalows on serene lakes, providing a unique and peaceful experience.

9. Treehouses and Eco-Lodges:

- For a more adventurous and eco-friendly experience, consider staying in treehouses or eco-lodges in places like the northern jungles of Thailand.

10. Unique Stays: - Thailand offers an array of unique accommodations, such as overwater bungalows, igloo-shaped rooms, and cliffside retreats.

11. Campsites: - Some national parks and natural areas offer camping facilities for outdoor enthusiasts. Camping is also an option on certain islands.

12. Airbnb and Home Sharing: - Airbnb and other home-sharing platforms provide various accommodation types, from private rooms to entire homes, giving you a chance to stay like a local.

When booking accommodations in Thailand, consider the location, proximity to attractions and activities, and the level of service and amenities that suit your travel style and budget. Thailand's diverse range of accommodation options ensures that every traveler can find a place that meets their needs and preferences.

Top Hotels

Here's a selection of some of the best hotels to consider for your visit to Thailand, covering various price ranges and destinations:

Bangkok:

1. **Mandarin Oriental, Bangkok:** This iconic luxury hotel offers classic elegance along the Chao Phraya River. It features excellent dining, spa services, and a serene riverside setting.

2. **The Siam:** A luxurious urban resort with a strong sense of Thai art and culture, this boutique hotel offers a unique experience in the heart of Bangkok.
3. **Siam Kempinski Hotel:** Located near the shopping district of Siam, this five-star hotel offers elegance and comfort. It boasts an impressive spa, fine dining options, and a prime location for exploring the city.

Chiang Mai:

4. **Four Seasons Resort Chiang Mai:** This stunning resort is set amidst lush rice terraces and offers top-tier service, beautiful accommodations, and an excellent spa.
5. **137 Pillars House:** A boutique luxury hotel, it's known for its beautiful teakwood suites and a tranquil atmosphere in the heart of Chiang Mai.

Phuket:

6. **Amanpuri:** Nestled in a coconut grove above Pansea Beach, Amanpuri is an ultra-luxurious resort known for its private pavilions, world-class service, and serene surroundings.
7. **The Surin Phuket:** This elegant beachfront resort offers stunning views of the Andaman Sea, white sandy beaches, and a relaxed atmosphere.

Koh Samui:

8. **Four Seasons Resort Koh Samui:** Overlooking the Gulf of Siam, this high-end resort provides luxurious villas, excellent dining, and top-notch spa facilities.

9. **Conrad Koh Samui:** Perched on a hillside, this luxury resort offers breathtaking views, infinity pools, and impeccable service.

Krabi:

10. **Rayavadee Krabi:** Set in the stunning Phranang Peninsula, this unique resort is accessible only by boat and offers luxurious pavilions amidst limestone cliffs.
11. **Phulay Bay, a Ritz-Carlton Reserve:** Located in the Andaman Sea, this Ritz-Carlton Reserve property offers ultimate luxury with private villas, a beautiful beach, and top-notch dining.

Northern Thailand:

12. **Anantara Golden Triangle Elephant Camp & Resort:** This unique luxury resort offers elephant experiences and overlooks the borders of Thailand, Myanmar, and Laos.

Islands and Beaches:

13. **Six Senses Yao Noi, Phang Nga Bay:** Set on a private island, this stunning resort offers overwater villas, breathtaking views, and a tranquil atmosphere.
14. **Soneva Kiri, Koh Kood:** A luxurious eco-resort, it provides stunning villas, a treetop dining pod, and a range of unique experiences on a pristine island.

Chapter 6: Cultural Activities in Thailand

Thailand boasts a rich and diverse culture with a long history deeply influenced by Buddhism, traditions, and royal customs. Visitors to Thailand have the opportunity to immerse themselves in various cultural activities that provide insights into the country's heritage. Here are some cultural activities and aspects of Thai culture that visitors can enjoy:

1. Temples and Buddhism:

- Explore some of the most revered temples in the country, such as Wat Pho (Temple of the Reclining Buddha) and Wat Phra Kaew (Temple of the Emerald Buddha) in Bangkok, as well as Wat Phra Singh in Chiang Mai. These temples showcase intricate architecture, beautiful Buddha statues, and religious rituals.

2. Almsgiving Ceremony (Tak Bat):

- Wake up early to observe or participate in the almsgiving ceremony where monks walk through the streets to receive offerings of food from devout locals. This tradition provides a glimpse into daily Buddhist life.

3. Traditional Thai Dance and Theater:

- Attend a traditional Thai dance or theater performance, such as Khon (masked dance drama) or Thai classical dance, to appreciate the beauty of Thai performing arts. The Apsara Theater in Bangkok is a popular venue for such shows.

4. Thai Cooking Classes:

- Participate in a Thai cooking class to learn about the country's cuisine and food culture. You can visit local markets to shop for ingredients and then prepare popular dishes like Pad Thai, Green Curry, and Tom Yum soup.

5. Floating Markets:

- Visit floating markets, such as Damnoen Saduak near Bangkok or Amphawa, to witness the traditional way of life and local commerce in action. You can take a boat ride, sample local snacks, and shop for handicrafts.

6. Hill Tribe Visits:

- Travel to the northern region to visit hill tribe villages, including the Karen, Akha, and Lisu tribes. These visits offer a glimpse into the distinct cultures and traditions of Thailand's ethnic minorities.

7. Loy Krathong and Songkran Festivals:

- If your visit aligns with Thai festivals, join in the celebrations. Loy Krathong, the Festival of Lights, and Songkran, the Thai New Year's water festival, are two of the most significant and enjoyable celebrations.

8. Traditional Thai Massage and Wellness:

- Experience a traditional Thai massage or spa treatment, which is deeply rooted in Thai culture. These practices promote relaxation, healing, and well-being.

9. Visit Royal Palaces:

- Explore royal palaces like the Grand Palace in Bangkok and the Summer Palace in Hua Hin. These sites provide insights into the monarchy's role in Thai culture and history.

10. Muay Thai Boxing: - Watch a Muay Thai (Thai boxing) match, which is the national sport of Thailand. You can attend matches in venues across the country, and even take lessons if you're interested in learning this martial art.

11. Arts and Crafts: - Shop for traditional Thai crafts, including silk products, wood carvings, ceramics, and intricate Thai-style artwork. Visit artisan workshops to see how these crafts are created.

12. Annual Elephant Festivals: - Attend one of the annual elephant festivals in Thailand, where you can witness parades, cultural performances, and activities that celebrate the historical connection between Thai people and elephants.

13. Royal Barge Procession: - If you visit during a special occasion, you might witness the grand Royal Barge Procession, which features elaborately decorated ceremonial boats and is an impressive display of Thai culture.

Thailand's culture is a fascinating blend of tradition, spirituality, and modernity. Visitors can engage in various cultural activities and experiences to gain a deeper appreciation of the country's heritage and way of life. It's essential to approach these activities with respect and an open mind to fully enjoy and understand Thai culture

Chapter 7:
Nightlife And Festivals In Thailand

Thailand has a vibrant and diverse nightlife scene that caters to a wide range of tastes and preferences. Whether you're looking for bustling nightclubs, laid-back beach parties, or cultural entertainment, you'll find plenty of options. Here are some of the best nightlife areas and experiences in Thailand:

1. Bangkok:

- Bangkok is Thailand's bustling capital and has a nightlife scene to match its reputation. The city offers something for everyone, from high-energy nightclubs in Sukhumvit to the more laid-back rooftop bars and jazz lounges. Khao San Road is a favorite among backpackers, known for its cheap drinks and street food. Sukhumvit Road is home to a wide range of nightspots, including bars, clubs, and lounges, while Asiatique The Riverfront provides a more refined experience with dining and cultural performances by the Chao Phraya River.

2. Pattaya:

- Pattaya is renowned for its vibrant nightlife, and Walking Street is the epicenter of this lively scene. This pedestrian-only street is lined with bars, nightclubs, go-go bars, and a party atmosphere that continues into the early hours. For a more relaxed experience, head to Pattaya's beachfront bars and lounges.

3. Phuket:

- Patong Beach in Phuket is a nightlife hotspot with the famous Bangla Road. It's known for its energetic and sometimes rowdy atmosphere, featuring countless bars, nightclubs, and go-go bars. For a more sophisticated nightlife experience, many beach clubs offer beachfront parties with excellent music and ocean views.

4. Chiang Mai:

- Chiang Mai's nightlife is relatively more tranquil compared to some other destinations, but it has a lot to offer. Nimmanhaemin Road is a trendy area popular with the local and expat community, known for its mix of bars, live music venues, and rooftop bars. Some places host open-mic nights and live band performances, creating a relaxed ambiance.

5. Pai:

- While Pai is generally known for its laid-back and serene atmosphere, it also has a small but active nightlife scene. The Pai Walking Street, lined with stalls selling street food, handcrafted items, and clothing, comes alive at night. Several bars and live music venues offer opportunities to unwind and meet fellow travelers.

6. Hua Hin:

- Hua Hin's nightlife is more family-friendly and laid-back. The night market is a popular evening spot, offering an array of street food, shopping, and live music. While there are bars in the area, the ambiance is generally more relaxed compared to the party destinations.

7. Isaan Region:

- The northeastern Isaan region offers a unique cultural experience. In towns and villages, you can find local bars with live music, often featuring traditional Thai instruments and dance performances. It's a great opportunity to immerse yourself in local culture and traditions.

8. Cultural Performances:

- Chiang Mai, in particular, is known for its traditional dance and music performances. These shows often take place during cultural dinners and showcase the grace and beauty of Thai culture. Khantoke Dinner &

Cultural Show is a popular choice where visitors can enjoy Northern Thai cuisine while being entertained by dance and music performances.

9. Festivals and Special Events:

- Some of Thailand's most unique nightlife experiences are found during festivals and special events. During Songkran, the Thai New Year, you'll experience massive water fights. The Full Moon Party on Koh Phangan is an internationally famous beach party featuring music, fire shows, and neon paint.

It's important to remember that Thailand's nightlife can vary greatly depending on the destination and even the specific areas within a city. The level of energy, the types of establishments, and the overall vibe can be quite different. Whether you prefer dancing until dawn or relaxing with a drink by the beach, Thailand has a nightlife scene to suit your style. Always exercise responsible behavior and be mindful of local customs and laws while enjoying the nightlife in Thailand.

Festivals

Thailand is known for its vibrant and diverse calendar of festivals and celebrations. Visitors to the country have the opportunity to immerse themselves in these colorful and culturally rich events. Here are some of the most notable feasts and festivals you can enjoy in Thailand:

1. Songkran (Thai New Year):

- Songkran is one of the most famous festivals in Thailand and is celebrated with water fights across the country. It typically falls in April and is a time of joy and cleansing. Visitors can participate in the water festivities, enjoy traditional ceremonies at temples, and witness parades and cultural performances.

2. Loy Krathong (Festival of Lights):

- Loy Krathong is celebrated on the full moon of the 12th month in the Thai lunar calendar (usually November). It involves releasing small, decorated boats (krathongs) into rivers and waterways to pay respects to the goddess of water. The sight of thousands of illuminated krathongs on the water is enchanting.

3. Yi Peng Lantern Festival:

- Held concurrently with Loy Krathong, the Yi Peng Lantern Festival takes place in Chiang Mai. It is famous for the release of thousands of sky lanterns into the night sky, creating a surreal and breathtaking sight.

4. Vegetarian Festival (Tesagan Gin Je):

- Celebrated primarily in Phuket and select areas, this festival occurs in October. Devotees and participants observe a strict vegetarian diet, wear white clothing, and engage in religious rituals. Visitors can witness colorful processions, martial arts displays, and the piercing of cheeks with sharp objects in a show of devotion.

5. Phi Ta Khon (Ghost Festival):

- This unique and quirky festival takes place in Dan Sai, Loei Province, typically in June or July. It involves participants dressing up as ghosts with colorful masks and costumes, accompanied by lively music and dancing. It's a playful and intriguing event.

6. Phi Ta Khon:

- Celebrated in July, Phi Ta Khon is a colorful ghost festival in Dan Sai, Loei Province. Participants wear elaborate masks and costumes, and the event features music, dancing, and parades.

7. Rocket Festival (Bun Bang Fai):

- Held in various regions, especially in the northeast of Thailand, this festival usually takes place in May. It involves the launching of large homemade rockets into the sky in an attempt to bring rain for the upcoming rice planting season.

8. Elephant Festival:

- The Elephant Festival in Surin, typically in November, features parades of beautifully decorated elephants, cultural performances, and sports events. It's a celebration of Thailand's deep connection with elephants.

9. King's Birthday and Father's Day:

- December 5th is celebrated as the King's Birthday and Father's Day in Thailand. It's an occasion for public celebrations, including lighting ceremonies and fireworks in honor of the king's birthday.

10. Rocket Festival (Bun Bang Fai): - Held in various northeastern provinces of Thailand, this festival coincides with the start of the rainy season (usually in May). It involves the launching of large bamboo rockets to encourage rainfall for agricultural purposes.

11. Coronation Day: - Celebrated in early May, Coronation Day marks the anniversary of the coronation of the Thai king. The event may include religious ceremonies and festivities in the capital and other major cities.

12. Nakhon Phanom Illuminated Boat Procession:

- Taking place in October or November, this festival in Nakhon Phanom sees beautifully illuminated boats floating down the Mekong River. The boats are decorated with intricate designs and often depict scenes from Buddhist and Hindu mythology.

13. Chiang Mai Flower Festival:

- Held in early February, the Chiang Mai Flower Festival showcases the region's rich floral diversity. Visitors can enjoy elaborate flower parades, beautifully decorated floats, and garden displays.

14. Phuket Old Town Festival:

- This annual event celebrates the history and culture of Phuket's Old Town. It features cultural performances, food vendors, street art, and a lively street fair.

15. Buffalo Racing Festival (Chonburi):

- This unique festival, held in Chonburi in October, features buffalo races along with traditional games and competitions. It's a fun and lively event that draws both locals and tourists.

16. Trang Underwater Wedding Ceremony:

- Taking place in February, this event in Trang features couples donning traditional Thai wedding attire and participating in underwater ceremonies amidst the coral reefs. It's a symbolic and unique celebration of love.

17. Surin Elephant Round-Up:

- Held in Surin in November, this festival showcases the region's strong bond with elephants. Visitors can watch elephant shows, races, and parades, providing insight into the cultural significance of these magnificent creatures.

18. Long-Neck Karen New Year:

- The Long-Neck Karen people celebrate their New Year in villages near Chiang Mai. Visitors have the opportunity to witness their unique customs, dances, and traditions.

19. King Taksin Festival (Tak):

- This festival in Tak, held in December, commemorates King Taksin the Great's victory over the Burmese. It includes reenactments, cultural performances, and food stalls.

20. Rocket Festival (Yasothon):

- Yasothon hosts one of the most famous rocket festivals in May. It features rocket launches, traditional music, and parades, as well as contests for the most impressive rockets.

Chapter 8:
Souvenirs And Shopping in Thailand

Shopping in Thailand is a vibrant and diverse experience, and the country is known for its markets, shopping centers, and unique items that cater to all budgets and tastes. Here are some areas and types of shopping visitors can enjoy in Thailand:

1. Street Markets:

- **Chatuchak Weekend Market, Bangkok:** This massive market covers about 35 acres and features over 15,000 stalls. You can find nearly anything here, from clothing, accessories, and home decor to vintage items, antiques, and even pets. It's an excellent place to discover unique souvenirs and enjoy the vibrant atmosphere.
- **Asiatique the Riverfront, Bangkok:** Set along the Chao Phraya River, this open-air night market

combines shopping, dining, and entertainment. You can shop for clothing, handicrafts, and souvenirs while enjoying live performances and river views.
- **Walking Street Markets, Chiang Mai:** Chiang Mai is a hub for street markets. The Sunday Walking Street, Saturday Walking Street, and Night Bazaar are among the most popular. These markets are ideal for shopping for local handicrafts, textiles, traditional art, and sampling delectable Northern Thai cuisine.
- **Pai Night Market:** The Pai Night Market offers a relaxed and bohemian shopping experience. It's known for its artistic and handcrafted items, including clothing, jewelry, and accessories. The market is the perfect place to soak up the town's laid-back atmosphere.

2. **Shopping Districts:**

- **Pratunam, Bangkok:** Pratunam is a bustling shopping district known for its wholesale clothing market. It's a haven for bargain shoppers, offering a wide selection of affordable clothing, accessories, and textiles. The Platinum Fashion Mall is a major attraction here.
- **Siam Square, Bangkok:** Siam Square is a youthful and trendy shopping district featuring a mix of fashion boutiques, unique designer shops, and art galleries. It's the place to find the latest fashion trends and street style.
- **CentralWorld, Bangkok:** CentralWorld is one of the largest shopping malls in Southeast Asia. It caters to all shopping preferences, from high-end designer brands to local shops and department stores. It also hosts cultural events and festivals.

- **Nimmanhaemin Road, Chiang Mai:** Nimmanhaemin Road is a vibrant and creative district in Chiang Mai. It's the go-to place for art, design, and fashion enthusiasts. Boutiques, art galleries, and cafés line the streets, offering a fusion of contemporary and traditional styles.

3. Shopping Malls:

- **Terminal 21, Bangkok:** Terminal 21 is a unique shopping mall with each floor themed after different world cities, complete with corresponding decor and items. You can find a variety of international and local brands, along with a range of dining options.
- **Emporium and EmQuartier, Bangkok:** These luxury shopping centers are located in the Sukhumvit area, catering to a more upscale clientele. They house high-end designer boutiques, gourmet dining, and impressive entertainment options.
- **Central Festival, Phuket:** Central Festival is the largest mall in Phuket, offering a broad range of shopping choices, from fashion and electronics to dining and entertainment. It's a great place to escape the sun and enjoy some retail therapy.

4. Traditional Markets:

- **Damnoen Saduak Floating Market:** Located not far from Bangkok, this market is famous for its traditional canal market, where vendors sell fresh produce, street food, clothing, and local products from long-tail boats. It's a unique and photogenic experience.

- **Warorot Market (Kad Luang), Chiang Mai:** Warorot Market is a bustling and historic market in the heart of Chiang Mai. It's a fantastic place to immerse yourself in local culture and shop for fresh produce, spices, traditional textiles, handicrafts, and souvenirs.

5. Handicraft Villages:

- **Bo Sang, Chiang Mai:** Bo Sang is renowned for its handmade paper umbrellas. Visitors can watch artisans craft these colorful parasols, which are used in festivals and celebrations. You can buy beautifully painted umbrellas and other traditional items.
- **Ban Tawai, Chiang Mai:** This village is famous for its woodcarvings and traditional Thai handicrafts. You can find intricately carved wooden items, furniture, and local crafts in the village's workshops and shops.

6. Night Markets:

- **Chiang Rai Night Bazaar:** This lively market features various stalls selling clothing, handicrafts, jewelry, and local food. It's an excellent place to shop for souvenirs and immerse yourself in the local night market culture.
- **Pattaya Night Bazaar:** Located along the beachfront, Pattaya's night market is known for a range of items, including clothing, electronics, gadgets, and street food. It's a bustling place to shop, dine, and enjoy the evening atmosphere.

Thailand's shopping scene is incredibly diverse, offering something for everyone. Whether you're interested in hunting for unique handicrafts, enjoying high-end retail therapy, or sampling delicious street food while browsing traditional markets, Thailand's shopping experiences are sure to leave you with memorable finds and a greater appreciation for the local culture.

Souvenirs

Thailand offers a wide variety of souvenirs that capture the essence of the country's rich culture, artistry, and natural beauty. Here are various souvenirs you can buy in Thailand:

1. Thai Silk:

- Thailand is renowned for its high-quality silk fabrics. You can purchase silk scarves, shawls, ties, and clothing in a range of vibrant colors and patterns. The Jim Thompson House in Bangkok is an excellent place to find authentic Thai silk.

2. Traditional Thai Clothing:

- Thai clothing is known for its intricate patterns and comfortable design. Traditional Thai outfits, including sarongs, fisherman pants, and hill tribe clothing, make for unique souvenirs.

3. Handcrafted Jewelry:

- Thai artisans create exquisite jewelry using semi-precious stones, silver, and gold. You can find beautifully designed rings, necklaces, bracelets, and earrings in jewelry shops and markets.

4. Thai Handicrafts:

- Thailand is famous for its handicrafts, such as hand-carved wooden items, hand-painted ceramics, intricate wooden masks, and lacquerware. You can find these in traditional markets and handicraft villages.

5. Thai Spa Products:

- Thailand is known for its traditional spa products. You can buy aromatic essential oils, herbal compress balls, and traditional massage tools to recreate a Thai spa experience at home.

6. Thai Art and Paintings:

- Thai art reflects the country's rich cultural heritage. You can purchase beautiful paintings, wall hangings, and sculptures depicting Thai landscapes, traditions, and Buddhism.

7. Thai Pottery and Ceramics:

- Thailand produces a wide range of pottery and ceramics, including intricately designed tea sets, vases, and dinnerware. Look for items with unique Thai patterns and designs.

8. Thai Elephant Products:

- While it's essential to be responsible and ethical in purchasing elephant-related items, you can find eco-friendly souvenirs such as elephant-themed artwork, clothing, and accessories. Consider supporting organizations that promote the conservation of elephants.

9. Thai Food Products:

- Thai cuisine is renowned worldwide, and you can bring the flavors of Thailand home by purchasing Thai spices, sauces, and ready-made curry pastes. Items like coconut milk, dried herbs, and rice are also popular choices.

10. Hill Tribe Crafts: - In the northern regions of Thailand, you can find souvenirs made by the local hill tribes, including handwoven textiles, jewelry, and handmade bags. Each tribe has its distinct style and patterns.

11. Traditional Thai Musical Instruments: - Thai musical instruments like bamboo flutes, xylophones, and gongs make unique and cultural souvenirs. They're not only decorative but can also be functional for music enthusiasts.

12. Thai Silk Parasols: - Thai silk parasols are beautifully decorated with intricate designs and patterns. They make for elegant and functional souvenirs and can serve as decorative pieces or sunshades.

13. Thai Decorative Items: - You can find a variety of decorative items, such as hand-painted plates, carved wooden figurines, and colorful lanterns, which can be great for adding a touch of Thai style to your home.

14. Amulets and Religious Artifacts: - Thailand is known for its reverence of Buddhism, and you can find Buddhist amulets and religious artifacts that are often blessed by monks. These can make meaningful souvenirs for spiritual travelers.

15. Thai Textiles and Fabrics: - Thai textiles, including traditional handwoven fabrics and batik, are available in a range of patterns and colors. They can be used for clothing, home decor, or as wall hangings.

When buying souvenirs in Thailand, it's essential to shop from reputable sources and support local artisans and ethical businesses. Also, be aware of the rules and regulations surrounding the export of certain items, especially those related to cultural heritage and wildlife.

Chapter 9:
Tips For Traveling in Thailand

Traveling in Thailand can be a rewarding and enriching experience. To make the most of your trip and ensure a smooth and enjoyable journey, consider these tips for travelers:

1. Respect Local Customs and Traditions:

- Thai culture places great emphasis on respect. Be mindful of local customs, such as removing your shoes before entering someone's home or a temple, and dressing modestly when visiting religious sites. Additionally, always show respect to the royal family and the monarchy.

2. Greet with the Wai:

- The traditional Thai greeting is called the "wai." To perform a wai, press your palms together and bow slightly. It's customary to return a wai when it's given to you. While not expected from tourists, showing respect through a wai is appreciated.

3. Learn Basic Thai Phrases:

- While many Thais in tourist areas speak English, learning a few basic Thai phrases can go a long way in making connections and showing respect. "Sawasdee" (hello) and "Kob Khun Ka/Krub" (thank you) are a good place to start.

4. Dress Appropriately:

- Dress modestly when visiting temples and religious sites. Women should cover their shoulders and knees, and both men and women should remove their shoes before entering temple buildings.

5. Be Mindful of Your Feet:

- In Thai culture, feet are considered the lowest part of the body and are considered dirty. Avoid pointing your feet at people or religious objects, and don't use your feet to touch or point at things.

6. Hydrate and Protect from the Sun:

- Thailand's tropical climate can be scorching, so stay hydrated and wear sunscreen. Drink bottled water and avoid ice in your drinks if you're concerned about water quality.

7. Respect the Monarchy:

- The Thai monarchy is held in high regard, and it's essential to show respect. Avoid any discussions or actions that may be interpreted as disrespectful to the royal family.

8. Be Cautious with Street Food:

- Thai street food is delicious, but it's essential to choose vendors that appear clean and busy. If you have a sensitive stomach, consider taking precautions like carrying antacids.

9. Bargain Respectfully:

- Bargaining is common in many markets, but do so respectfully and with a smile. Don't haggle too aggressively, as this can be seen as disrespectful.

10. Use Local Transportation: - Consider using local transportation options like tuk-tuks, songthaews, and motorbike taxis to get around. They're often more affordable than traditional taxis.

11. Carry Cash and Small Change: - While credit cards are widely accepted in major cities, having cash is useful, especially in more remote areas. Carry small denominations for convenience.

12. Mind Your Trash: - Help preserve Thailand's natural beauty by disposing of your trash properly. Use designated bins and avoid littering.

13. Travel Insurance: - Always have travel insurance that covers medical emergencies. Medical care in Thailand is excellent, but it can be costly for foreigners without insurance.

14. Stay Aware of Scams: - Be cautious of scams, especially in tourist areas. Common scams may include overcharging for tuk-tuk rides or gem scams. Research common scams and stay vigilant.

15. Check Visa Requirements: - Verify visa requirements for your nationality before traveling to Thailand. Overstaying your visa can result in fines or deportation.

16. Respect the Environment: - When visiting natural areas like national parks, be respectful of the environment. Don't disturb wildlife, stay on designated paths, and avoid damaging coral reefs when snorkeling or diving.

17. Explore Beyond Tourist Hotspots: - While popular destinations are worth a visit, don't forget to explore off-the-beaten-path areas to experience the real Thailand and connect with local communities.

Thailand is known for its hospitality, and by showing respect for the culture and local customs, you can have a truly memorable and enjoyable travel experience. Enjoy the incredible cuisine, stunning landscapes, and the warmth of the Thai people while being a responsible and respectful traveler.

Conclusion

Thailand is a captivating and diverse destination that offers a wealth of experiences for travelers. Whether you're drawn to its rich culture, stunning natural landscapes, vibrant street markets, or delicious cuisine, Thailand has something for everyone. By respecting local customs and traditions, learning some basic Thai phrases, and practicing responsible tourism, you can fully immerse yourself in the beauty and warmth of Thai culture.

Exploring beyond the well-trodden tourist hotspots will reveal the authentic heart of the country, where you can connect with local communities and create lasting memories. From the bustling streets of Bangkok to the tranquil beaches of Phuket, from the historic temples of Chiang Mai to the lush jungles of the north, Thailand's diverse offerings will leave you with a deep appreciation for this incredible destination.

As you journey through the Land of Smiles, remember to try the delectable street food, purchase unique and meaningful souvenirs, and stay hydrated under the tropical sun. Thailand's enchanting charm, coupled with the warmth and friendliness of its people, will make your visit an unforgettable adventure.

Made in the USA
Middletown, DE
20 December 2023

46535584R00066